D1234616

Inside the Multi-Generational Family Business

A FAMILY
BUSINESS
PUBLICATION

Family Business Publications are the combined efforts of the Family Business Consulting Group and Palgrave Macmillan. These books provide useful information on a broad range of topics that concern the family business enterprise, including succession planning, communication, strategy and growth, family leadership, and more. The books are written by experts with combined experiences of over a century in the field of family enterprise and who have consulted with thousands of enterprising families the world over, giving the reader practical, effective, and time-tested insights to everyone involved in a family business.

FBCG, founded in 1994, is the leading business consultancy exclusively devoted to helping family enterprises prosper across generations.

Inside the
Multi-Generational
Family Business

*Nine Symptoms of Generational
Stack-Up and How to Cure Them*

Mark T. Green

palgrave
macmillan

First published in 2011 by
PALGRAVE MACMILLAN®
in the United States—a division of St. Martin's Press LLC,
175 Fifth Avenue, New York, NY 10010.

Where this book is distributed in the UK, Europe and the rest of the world,
this is by Palgrave Macmillan, a division of Macmillan Publishers Limited,
registered in England, company number 785998, of Houndmills,
Basingstoke, Hampshire RG21 6XS.

Palgrave Macmillan is the global academic imprint of the above companies
and has companies and representatives throughout the world.

Palgrave® and Macmillan® are registered trademarks in the United States,
the United Kingdom, Europe and other countries.

ISBN: 978–0–230–11184–4

Library of Congress Cataloging-in-Publication Data

Green, Mark T., 1964–
    Inside the Multi-Generational Family Business : Nine Symptoms of
Generational Stack-Up and How to Cure Them / Mark Green.
        p. cm.—(A family business publication)
    Includes bibliographical references and index.
    ISBN 978–0–230–11184–4 (alk. paper)
    1. Family-owned business enterprises—Management.
    2. Intergenerational relations. I. Title.

HD62.25.G74 2011
658'.045—dc22   2010036899

A catalogue record of the book is available from the British Library.

Design by Newgen Imaging Systems (P) Ltd., Chennai, India.

First edition: April 2011

10 9 8 7 6 5 4 3 2 1

Printed in the United States of America.

*To my generational heroes, sources of
inspiration, and loves:*

*Danielle (Millennial)
Karen (Gen X)
Mom (Silent Generation)
Grandma & Grandpa Vidas and
Great Uncle Kazys Grinius (Before there
were fancy names for generations)*

Contents

Foreword

Running a business can be one of the best things a family can experience: working together to build, maintain, and enhance a company that may have been in the family for generations or was just started in the current generation. However, business problems and family problems can turn into one and the same in any family company. As a family business consultant, I've seen that to hold true regardless of the business's size, age, industry, performance, number of family members/generations involved, and any other variable.

What Is Generational Stack-Up?

With this book, my goal is to help families understand and address a core problem they all experience, many without even realizing it. It's what I call "generational stack-up," or the tendency for family members from different generations to clash due to their discrepant values, mindsets, and approaches. One of the biggest issues family businesses face is problematic interactions between generations. This is often seen between the founding generation and second generation, or between the generation currently in power and the next, framed mainly as an issue of working across two generations or transferring the business from one to the next by dealing effectively with succession and ownership issues.

Those are, of course, important challenges for family businesses to overcome. But generational stack-up is far broader than that. Due to better healthcare technology and nutritional options, people are living longer, and due to shifting psychology and social trends, people are working much longer. Put those together, and you can realistically have as many as *five* generations involved in a family business, or 10 pairings and many more multi-generation combinations. The result: chaos, conflict and, not surprisingly, poor business performance, along with disrupted relationships. Stack-up goes well beyond two generations working together or one generation transferring the business to the next. It's about getting all the parts of the system to work together, in harmony, starting with shorter period and moving to much longer ones—ideally to perpetuity.

In working with hundreds of family businesses as an educator and consultant, part of my job has been to help them understand that the challenges and conflicts they face are normal, and that taking on everything at once is usually a recipe for failure. Instead, I help them break the challenges down into smaller, more manageable pieces. One effective way to do that is by seeing the conflicts as related to generational stack-up. To understand stack-up myself (having faced it in my own family business), I've explored research and insights from fields including biology, demography, neurobiology, psychology, sociology, gender studies, and of course management, entrepreneurship, and family business. Many time I use insights I've gained from these fields with family business clients to help them understand their situation and challenges.

An analogy I use with many family businesses to help them understand the nature of stack up is a medical one—specifically, thinking about stack-up as a "syndrome," or a cluster of symptoms that tend to occur together. Look at the list of items below and try to guess what they represent:

- Sadness
- Poor appetite
- Lack of enjoyment
- Feelings of guilt or worthlessness
- Sleeping too much or too little
- Trouble concentrating

- Significant weight loss or gain
- Low energy

If you guessed these are symptoms of working in a multi-generation family business, you get partial credit. Too often, they are. But they are also symptoms associated with the psychiatric disorder of depression. Importantly, in a given case of depression, not all symptoms need be present. Also importantly, viewing these groups of symptoms as representing the same disorder helps psychiatrists and others develop treatments for the condition.

In the same way, stack-up in family businesses can be considered a syndrome including several symptoms from a larger set, not all of which need be present in a given case. And just like for depression, treating stack-up first involves identifying its symptoms. The heart of the book is a discussion of each of nine stack-up symptoms and how to treat them.

What Can You Get out of This Book?

This book does not have all of the answers, but rather is a guide aimed at helping real family businesses and their professional advisors deal with the complexity and challenges of merging business with family. By understanding the trends driving generational stack-up and the mutually reinforcing symptoms that it involves, families will gain practical tools that help them navigate their relationships and how these affect the business, enabling them not only to survive but to *thrive* at home, the office, and the boardroom.

What's more, by taming generational stack-up using the tools in this book and others they may develop on their own, business families will improve their relationships—and business performance—while laying the groundwork for future generations to have greater harmony as well.

Acknowledgments

I would first like to acknowledge the families, businesses, owners, managers, advisors, employees, and students who inhabit the world of family business. A life of living, breathing, and working with family business has kept me learning, thinking, and always inspired.

I would like to thank my colleagues at the Family Business Consulting Group (FBCG) for their support and dedication to developing new ideas that can be of practical use to family businesses. Thanks to John Ward, Craig Aronoff, and the entire stable of FBCG authors and co-authors for their leadership and commitment to the continued craft of writing to help. I would also like to thank Leon and Katy Danco for blazing the trail in the world of family business—I will always remember the days of talking shop at your wonderful home.

I would especially like to thank Ken and Joan Austin for developing the Austin Family Business Program at Oregon State University and acknowledge my good fortune to have led the program for many years. It was their vision, along with the support and leadership of Jim Coleman, Pat Frishkoff, Ken Madden, Lori Luchak, Jim Kennedy, Rick Steinfeld, Greg Waggoner, Jim Baumgartner, Craig Chambers, Dave DeLap and so many others that I can't even begin to thank, that gave me the opportunity to work with so many family businesses and learn so much from them.

Special thanks to Emily, Michael, and Alice Powell of Powell's Books for providing the opportunity to learn about and enjoy your family and business.

A big thanks to my friend Michael Roth for his collection of one-liners on family business and support of this project. The nickels are piling up for using your material, and I will repay you shortly.

The best mentors in life aren't planned or assigned; they come from people willing to share their time and wisdom, even with those who aren't always willing to listen. I have had the good fortune of being around wonderful mentors who lead and inspire by teaching, writing, thinking, and helping others everyday. Their example, work habits, support, encouragement, and even the occasional, much-needed kick in the pants are even more appreciated today. Thanks again to Fred Thompson, Steve Maser, Tom Borcherding, Larry Jones, Gary Levine, George Raveling, and Jim McDiarmid for your example and guidance. I only hope to be able to pass on your wisdom to others.

To Sachin Waikar, who has not only made this book possible, but is by far the most valuable writing and editing partner I could hope for. I look forward to many years of collaboration. Thanks again for all of your support and diligence.

To the great folks at Palgrave Macmillan, especially Executive Editor Laurie Harting for her enthusiasm for and guidance of this project. Thanks also to Tiffany Huford and Kristy Lilas for their work.

Thanks to Sharri Dowling, my faithful assistant, for all her support, patience, and dedication.

Finally, a huge thanks to my family for their support, encouragement, and sacrifices in making this book possible.

I

The Syndrome of
Generational Stack-Up

L ess than 10 percent of family businesses make it past a
second generation.¹ But some of the 90-plus percent that
don't might consider themselves lucky.

Why?

Because multi-generational business families today face
unprecedented challenges working together. They're saddled,
often without even knowing it, with "generational stack-up,"
or the convergence of several generations as owners, managers, employees, and shareholders. Not surprisingly, each
generation has its own work style, biases, and approach to
money and business. And that causes conflict within and
across generations. Aging GI generation, born from 1905 to
1924, and Silent generation family members cling to CEO
positions and old-fashioned, status quo thinking while their
Boomer children deny the very possibility of retirement.
Gen X parents "helicopter" around their Gen Y children (also
known as Millennials), doing everything for them, then get
frustrated when Millennials show little ambition, independence, or skill regarding the family business. And everyone
wonders why running a business together causes so many
problems—on both professional and personal levels.

This chapter introduces the concept of generational
stack-up and discusses how thinking about stack-up as a
"syndrome," or cluster of symptoms, that business families

face can help you begin to treat this problem in your family and business. My goal is to help you not just survive stack-up, but to thrive in the face of it.

To begin to understand patterns related to stack-up, let's take a look at the Brown family of Brown Industrials, and the multiple stack-up symptoms they face.

The Unhappiest Place on Earth

"Stop, Uncle Ben!" Joey yelled. "Please stop!"

The "happiest place on earth" was far from it. As Uncle Ben gave eight-year-old Joey one of his patented pink bellies—slaps to his bare midsection—and Joey's screams became louder and louder, everyone from Joey's father and mother, George Brown III and Judy, to his aunt Ellen, to his grandfather, George Jr., begged Ben to stop. Unfortunately, the theatrics, which quickly escalated to name-calling and a near-scuffle, happened poolside at a Disneyworld resort in Orlando, Florida, in full view of many of the family's fellow attendees at the 2008 Association of Midwest Manufacturers meeting. The only good thing was that 84-year-old George Brown Sr., the family business founder and patriarch, and his wife, Lucy, missed the excitement because they were at the resort's spa. But George Sr. and Lucy heard all about it that evening when the extended family sat down for a long, heated discussion of the multiple deep grievances—business-related and personal—among members that had helped motivate the pink-belly incident. All the issues were part of the complex dynamics behind the scenes at Brown Industrials, the third-generation business George Sr. had started nearly six decades earlier.

No one could have predicted how challenging family relationships would become—or how successful Brown Industrials would be—when George Sr. started manufacturing farm-machine parts from a small downstate Illinois shop soon after returning from service in World War II. As Brown Industrials grew into a respected regional manufacturer supplying the farming, automotive, and trucking industries, George Sr.'s family expanded as well; he married his high-school sweetheart, Mary, around the time he started the company, and the couple had three children over the next few years.

See figure 1.1 for the full family tree.

By the time their eldest, George Jr., was a teenager, George Sr. and Mary had divorced. Within a year, George Sr. married Lucy, a secretary at Brown Industrials who was closer to George Jr.'s age than to his own. Ben, George Sr. and Lucy's only child, was born when George Jr. was 15 years old. George Jr. showed an immediate knack for the business, helping with finance and operations even while in college. After completing an accounting degree, he became the only one of his three full siblings to join the business, rising quickly from finance manager to vice president of finance to president, marrying Linda and having two children of his own along the way. Linda, who also held an accounting degree, worked for an accounting firm for several years but turned down a faster-than-average promotion to manager to

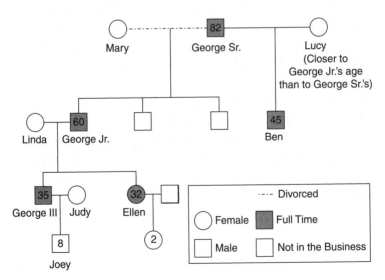

Figure 1.1   The Syndrome of Generational Stack-Up: The Brown Family

stay home with their children, George III and Ellen, as her husband's responsibilities grew.

George Jr. wasn't George Sr.'s only child to join Brown Industrials, which had become a $50-million-dollar operation by the 1970s. After much cajoling by George Sr.'s second wife, Lucy, the business founder agreed to have their son Ben join the business soon after he dropped out of college during his freshman year to pursue an acting career (which never materialized). Ben started in the sales department, where his sometimes-ribald humor helped him build customer relationships. "Customers love him," George Sr. pointed out as he promoted Ben repeatedly, ultimately to VP of sales. George Jr. pointed out that some customers were put off by Ben's jokes and casual approach, and that his half-sibling's devotion to customers often took the form of luxurious golf trips and other outings around the country—boondoggles that cost the company in terms of both large entertainment bills and Ben's long absences.

George Jr., on the other hand, found himself working increasingly long hours, sometimes to cover for Ben, and always under the watchful eye of George Sr., who even as he moved into his 80s and battled complications from diabetes kept a hand seemingly in everything from the smallest customer contracts to the simplest office-space requests, often pestering George Jr. about these issues through written memos and phone calls—always with the mantra of "got to minimize risk, son." By the time of the pink-belly incident, George Jr. longed for the more flexible life he saw Ben leading; at 60 and with money in the bank, George Jr. could have considered retirement in the near future, and loved the idea of learning to paint, but would have been hard-pressed to convince his father of the value of that. It was also hard for him to imagine not earning money anymore. And George Jr. knew that George Sr. had him in mind to succeed him as CEO, but the elder Brown never brought up succession. As he looked back at his life, George Jr. felt that by giving up so much for work—including time with his kids George III and Ellen—he'd become just like his father. But he couldn't imagine making a near-future break from the company where he'd spent nearly four decades.

Ironically, after his children graduated from college, George Jr. spent more time with them than ever before—because they joined Brown Industrials. By the time of the Disneyworld trip, George III (35 years old) was the operations manager and Ellen (32 years old) worked as a sales manager. Both enjoyed their work and were good at it. At the same time, both faced significant challenges. George III, who was expected to follow in his father's footsteps and eventually serve as president, found himself increasingly torn between his professional responsibilities and home life. He had promised himself he'd spend more time with eight-year-old Joey, but was letting work meetings and conferences keep him from baseball games, Cub Scout meetings, and parent–teacher conferences. "I need you at home more," his wife Judy, a teacher with her own busy schedule, frequently reminded him, wanting both parents to be present at as many of Joey's activities as possible. George III's father and grandfather weren't much help: George Sr. made clear that "work must come first," and while his father, George Jr., was generally supportive, he tended not to speak up against George Sr. and had set a clear example of living his father's value of work first. Given the circumstances, it was hard for George III to imagine taking any time for himself, though he occasionally managed to sneak away to the gym or to play guitar with his friends. Overall, he seemed to be living the song "Stuck in the Middle."

Ellen, George III's sister, arguably had it even worse. Mother of a two-year-old and married to a management consultant who traveled almost every week for work, Ellen returned from hectic days at Brown Industrials or short out-of-town trips to customers to spend her evenings managing a daughter fully into the terrible twos and then collapsing on the sofa in front of the TV. It didn't help that her boss was Uncle Ben, who often took advantage of her dedication by handing her last-minute work and sending her on sales calls he was supposed to make. It also didn't help that her mother, Linda, went out of her way to remind Ellen that she had given up a promising career to stay home with Ellen and George III, and that "women these days seem to think they can have it all." According to Linda, they couldn't.

Given these family dynamics, many of them revolving around Uncle Ben, it's no surprise that the pink-belly incident quickly deteriorated into name-calling and accusations beside the Disneyworld pool. When the family sat down to talk that evening, they knew they were angry. They also knew, from previous experience, that talking about their problems with one another might smooth things over for weeks or even months, but that the same patterns would remain, with conflict rising again.

What the Brown family probably didn't know is that many of the problems they faced stemmed from "generational stack-up"—or the challenge individuals from multiple generations face when trying to work together, due to their clashing experiences and values. Some of the patterns in the Browns' story fit into stack-up–related "symptoms" I call "Control beyond the Grave," "Boomer Retirement Mirage," "Generation-Straddling Sibs," and "Who's Your Daddy?"

This book aims to help family-business owners like the Browns, and those who work with them, understand the origins of generational stack-up, what the symptoms look like, and how to treat them, creating much more harmonious family and professional relationships, as well as enhanced business performance.

Generational Stack-Up: What Is It and How Did We Get Here?

Generational stack-up is behind many of the problems modern family businesses face. To help explain, I'll use an analogy and point to sources of the problem.

Stack-Up and the Tower of Babel

Remember the Tower of Babel from the Book of Genesis? The tower, constructed by descendants of Noah after the flood, was to be a heaven-reaching city in which all of humankind could live in harmony, rather than scattering across the world and living in separate groups. Originally meant to honor God, the structure was to be built by all of earth's people, but, as the story goes, the builders lost sight of their mission partway through, and erected the tower to glorify Man, not God.

Naturally, God didn't appreciate this. As punishment, he made it such that all the tower's builders spoke different languages. Paralyzed by this move from one language to many, the people abandoned the tower project and did exactly what they'd hoped to avoid: they scattered across the globe, forming tribes around different languages and customs, never again to enjoy a truly united humanity.

In many ways, our modern lives mirror the Tower of Babel. This is in part because we speak different languages and have different cultures and customs worldwide, which sometimes leads to clashes. But even in countries where we all speak the same language, we often struggle to communicate. Much of this is due to generational differences—people born in different generations tend to have different values and worldviews, including attitudes toward work and family. As more and more generations get stacked up on top of one another, these discrepant "languages" lead to conflicts in multiple areas.

Nowhere are the effects of stack-up more apparent than in family businesses, as demonstrated by the embattled Browns of Brown Industrials. When George Jr. and others struggle against George Sr.'s over-controlling management style, that's largely because of generational differences: George Sr., who grew up during the post-Depression era, believed he had to wring out all risk from the business, and thus tried to keep a hand in even the smallest details. When George III and his sister Ellen wrestle with maintaining a work-life balance—including dealing with parents who don't understand this challenge and even dismiss it—it's largely because of generational differences: the third-generation Browns, now in their 30s, belong to an era of unprecedented choices and flexibility regarding careers and home lives, a mixed blessing leading to much heartache and intergenerational conflict.

Thus family businesses resemble mini Towers of Babel in many ways. Each family has built its "tower" with the hope that it will last for generation after generation, stretching to eternity. But because each generation of family business members speaks a different language—based on discrepant values and approaches to work, money, and family—they struggle to collaborate, often clashing, until parts of the tower crumble or the whole thing tumbles. To be sure, such conflicts happen in nonfamily firms as well, but the stakes are highest for family firms, where stack-up-related problems affect almost every aspect of members' lives, rather than being limited primarily to the workplace.

What's more, stack-up is a problem in family businesses worldwide, across industries. The specific generation-based values and patterns may differ from country to country, but the core issue is the same. I've seen stack-up symptoms from Montana to Mumbai, from small family farms to giant publishing houses. The bottom line is that unless members of different generations learn to speak the same language and try to understand one another, they're destined to clash repeatedly, and diminish the firm's value, along with their relationships and quality of life.

How Did We Get Here?

So how did stack-up become such a big problem in general and for family businesses specifically?

Among the reasons are:

We're living longer. It's no surprise that we live much longer today than in the past. The median age of individuals in the United States more than doubled (from 16 years to 35 years) from 1820 to 2000.[2] The average life expectancy for U.S. residents is now just under 78 years, an increase of nearly 30 years over that figure for the developed world in 1950.[3] But what may be most surprising is how many people are living longer than ever before: the United States has the greatest number of centenarians (the over-100 crowd), an estimated 96,548 in late 2008, one of the country's fastest-growing demographics.[4] Longer lives mean more space for generations to stack up on each other.

We're working to an older age. Positive and negative trends have contributed to our working to a much later average age than before. Enhanced medical technologies are allowing us to maintain a higher quality of life well into our 70s and 80s, which means we can continue showing up at the office later in life. At the same time, trends in retirement plans and savings are forcing many to work past historically typical retirement ages. Although the typical American still retires at 63, many will have to work until closer to 70 to enjoy sufficient retirement income, partly because of decreasing Social Security benefits.[5] So it's no surprise these days to see articles like "Six Ways for Older Workers to Impress Hiring Managers" and "Finding a New Job after 50."[6] Moreover, many people who don't have to continue working, especially in family businesses, *choose* to do so for a variety of reasons, which we'll get into a bit later.

We're building more family businesses. In the United States, there are an estimated 24 million family firms.[7] These vary from regional companies to multibillion-dollar giants, from true mom-and-pops to household names like Levi Strauss, S.C. Johnson, and the *New York Times.* Family-owned businesses tend to perform better than nonfamily firms on key indicators, including profitability, as suggested by multiple U.S.-based and international studies.[8] There isn't much research yet, but this trend of superior performance seems to be continuing amidst the current economic slump, as family businesses tend to be more focused on long-term growth and strategies.

Fast Fact

U.S. family businesses account for over half of the country's workforce and nearly two thirds of the Gross Domestic Product (GDP).

Source: Among articles citing statistics like these are F. de Visscher and M. Bruel (1994), "The adolescence of the American family business," *Family Business Newsletter*, Volume 9.

These trends have driven unprecedented generational stack-up in general and in family businesses specifically, such that up to five generations may work together. Of course, many of these trends point to good things: we're living longer, healthier lives and using family businesses to create more profits and even contribute more to the global economy. But due to discrepant values, experiences, and worldviews, we're also clashing in unprecedented ways across generations, diminishing the value we create and disrupting our quality of life.

The Stacked-Up Generations

Who are the stacked-up generations in U.S. family businesses? They represent a diverse crew, ranging from World War II veterans to Guitar Hero–playing 20-somethings, from Gen X soccer and hockey moms who work part-time to Boomers with one foot in retirement.

Here are snapshots of the five U.S. generations stacked up on each other, based on a convergence of definitions in the media. See *The Stacked-up Generations at a Glance* table for a summary. Note that as I write this, there is growing consensus that the current Gen Y or Millennial generation is coming to a close, with a sixth generation on the horizon. Imagine that, six generations stacked up together, sometimes in the same house or in the same business.

The GI Generation (1905–1924). Born at the beginning of the twentieth century, the youngest GI generation members are now in their 80s. But many are still going strong, including at work. They survived the U.S.'s Great Depression and many wars; members of this generation and its successor Silent generation (see below) served three times more years in the military, on average, than any other before or since.[9] Because they went through these events, GIs have a strong focus on stability; they are loyal to a fault, patriotic, and believe strongly in the institutions of God, work, and family, working relentlessly to preserve these. They respect authority. GIs—including many true GIs returning from World War II—had many children, helping drive the Baby Boom that gave us Boomers (see below). In the Brown Industrials case, George Brown Sr. is on the cusp of the GI generation and the one that came after it, the Silent generation, adding to his focus on maintaining strict control over all aspects of the business and minimizing risk.

The Silent Generation (1925–1944). Like the GIs, the Silent generation's values and worldview were shaped largely by the Depression and wars, helping generate their focus on living modestly to save money and ensuring that their families stay intact. Their influencing events also helped make this the smallest generation by size (hence its name). Some served in World War II and some served in the thankless Korean War. They had a smaller crop of children than the GI generation, consisting of late Boomers and Gen Xers. And they started or joined a number of family businesses. In many industries today, this is the owning class. For example, Silent generation members still preside over many U.S. farming, timber, and manufacturing operations. Like their preceding generation, they are often uncomfortable discussing money, death, and succession, and they prefer face-to-face communication and having things on paper over phone calls and e-mails. George Brown Sr. is on the cusp of this generation and his second wife, Lucy, is squarely within it, contributing to their willingness to include Ben in the business to help preserve the family.

Baby Boomers (1946–1964). Baby Boomers, or Boomers, are perhaps the most-discussed generation in the media, partly because they were born out of the post–World War II celebration and partly because they have just reached retirement, taxing the U.S. Social Security system; Boomer actor Dennis Hopper (of *Easy Rider* fame) was even a retirement-plan pitchman shortly before his death in 2010. Having grown up with Elvis, Vietnam, Woodstock, and Watergate, Boomers rebelled against their parents and other authorities with sex, drugs, and rock and roll. Many then returned to their *Leave it to Beaver* roots, essentially becoming richer versions of their parents, with large amounts of acquired wealth. Partly because of this, Boomers also have the highest rates of divorce and multiple families. And they count among them the first of the "rock-star entrepreneurs," for example Bill Gates and Phil Knight. The tendency to be of many minds carries over to Boomers' mentality about retirement—they want to live a more leisurely life, including hobbies and giving back, but it's hard for them to imagine not working. So, in general, they try to have it all, then wonder why it seems like they don't. George Jr. and his wife Linda are squarely in the Boomer generation, while half-sibling Ben is on the cusp of Boomers and Gen X. This helps explain some of the struggles they go through balancing family, money, career, and other aspects of their identities.

Generation X (1965–1980). Gen X is probably one of the most publicly beaten-up generations, in terms of where they came from and where they're going. That may not be surprising, given that Gen X came of age when traditional structures—the Berlin Wall, the Soviet Union, the nuclear family, the department store, the lifelong company job—were crumbling, replaced by a new globalism replete with instant communication (including the Internet), downsizing, malls, outsourcing, and relentless pursuit of efficiency. Opportunities and threats became hard to distinguish. Out of this chaos grew Gen X's skepticism and self-reliance; many rejected working for conventional companies, spawning a large crop of successful entrepreneurs, many building

Internet-based businesses (e.g., Amazon's Jeff Bezos), following in the footsteps of high-tech icons like Bill Gates and Steve Jobs. However, without clear traditional frameworks for their careers, families, and identities, members of Gen X struggle to balance work with everything else, often feeling like they're failing in every role. George III and his wife Judy are squarely in Gen X, giving context to some of their struggles with work-life balance.

Generation Y (1981–2009). Most Gen Y members, or Millennials, have come of age since the turn of the century, their identities molded by ubiquitous technology including cell phones, iPods, and instant messaging. They don't talk, they chat. They don't turn pages, they click. Their public library is the World Wide Web. They're famous for short attention spans. Their ranks include celebrities from Chelsea Clinton to LeBron James to Miley Cyrus. They've seen the instant fame that reality TV bestows. They've also been included more deeply in family decision making than any other generation, on everything from what restaurants to eat at to what car the family should buy, leading to a healthy sense of inclusiveness that they bring to work; they're about collaboration, not control. Unfortunately, this same trend has led to Boomer and Gen X parents doing too much for their Gen Y kids, rather than letting them figure things out on their own, spawning the terms "helicopter" and "hothouse" parents, and leading to the labeling of the United States today as a "nation of wimps."[10] As a result, Gen Y members, many just entering the workplace, represent a curious blend of confidence, pragmatism, and lack of initiative, sometimes generating more ideas than actual work, and job-hopping relentlessly. As one observer puts it, "...they change the workplace by quitting, rather than complaining....Gen Y at large feels uncomfortable being openly confrontational."[11] To complicate matters, Gen Y faces the bleakest economic environment since the Great Depression: the global downturn that began in 2008 has led to the highest levels of unemployment among those between the ages of 16 and 24 since the middle of the twentieth century.[12] On top of that, this generation is expected to bear much of the strain that previous generations are placing on the U.S. economy: over 10,000 Boomers will become eligible for Social Security and Medicare *daily* for the next 20 years.[13] In the Brown Industrials case, eight-year-old Joey is from Gen Y, and his parents' deep involvement in his life may have implications for him down the road, especially if he joins the family business.

Stacked-up Generations at a Glance

Generation	Motto	Influencers	Attitude toward Work	Attitude toward Family
GI (1905–1924)	"Save for a rainy day"	• Great Depression • World War II	• Respect for authority and hierarchy • Minimizing risk, even if that means giving up profits • No discussion of succession	• Deeply loyal • Focus on preserving family relationships
Silent (1925–1945)	"Live within your means"	• Great Depression • Multiple wars	• More balanced view of risk-reward, but conservative overall • Prefer face-to-face discussion and having things on paper	• Very civic-minded; wanted family to be strong part of community • Focus on preserving family relationships
Boomers (1946–1964)	"We can have it all"	• Vietnam • Watergate • Woodstock	• Rejection of traditional authority and hierarchy • Strong materialism • Struggle with idea of retirement	• Rejected parents' models of stable family • Highest divorce and multiple family rates

Continued

Continued

Generation	Motto	Influencers	Attitude toward Work	Attitude toward Family
Gen X (1965–1980)	"Do it yourself"	• Cold War • Reaganomics • Video games • Internet	• Skeptical of traditional models of work • Strong entrepreneurial spirit • Struggle with work-life balance	• Skeptical of traditional models of family • High rate of divorce and multiple families
Gen Y (1981–2009)	"Do it for us"	• Internet, cell phones • Tech Boom • Reality TV	• Collaboration, not control • Non-confrontational • Lots of ideas, too little progress	• Not parent and child, but partners • Expect Mom and Dad to do it for them

The Syndrome of Stack-Up, Its Symptoms, and Treatment

Now that you have an understanding of the phenomenon of generational stack-up in family businesses, the trends driving it, and the specific generations involved, let's look at its symptoms and how to treat them. To do that, we have to think of stack-up as a "syndrome" or cluster of symptoms that tend to show up together. Not every case of stack-up has the same symptoms, but all cases have at least one.

So what are the symptoms of stack-up?

The Symptoms of Stack-Up

My work with family business clients across the United States and discussions with colleagues—professors, attorneys, bankers, fellow consultants, and others—who deal daily with family businesses suggests several patterns, or symptoms, related to stack-up. In this case, symptoms aren't necessarily located within a given family member (though they may originate in one person, as a result of their generation status), but represent problems with the system of relationships among members.

I created the symptom list below based on the patterns I've observed most frequently in family businesses. The symptoms are ordered based on which generations they tend to affect the most, from oldest to youngest (see table below, which also reflects the order of the chapters focused on these symptoms). Of course, most symptoms affect multiple generations, at least indirectly, including those not marked in the table below. Note also that this list is not meant to be exhaustive, but it certainly covers the most common patterns I've observed.

	Generations Affected				
Symptom	GI	Silent	Boomer	Gen X	Gen Y
Control beyond the Grave	X	X	X	X	
Who's Your Daddy?	X	X	X	X	
Battle of the Super-Women		X	X	X	
Meet the MEOWs		X	X	X	
Boomer Retirement Mirage		X	X	X	
My Child, My Boss			X	X	
Generation-Straddling Sibs			X	X	X
Overbalanced Gen X			X	X	X
WimpY Gen Y			X	X	X

Control beyond the Grave. As mentioned earlier, members of the Silent and GI generations have been through a lot—an economic depression, several wars, and a booming global economy. Many of them have nurtured their

"babies"—children and businesses—through these challenging and exciting times. While the legacy of earlier generations is often a very positive and valuable influence for a
family business, by clinging excessively to control through
life and, yes, even after death (through contracts and other
legacies), these cohorts can stifle the growth of later generations and the business. In the Brown Industrials case, George
Sr.'s behavior and its consequences for others exemplifies
this symptom, as the eldest Brown keeps a hand in even the
smallest details of the business despite his status as an octo-
genarian with diabetes.

Who's (or What's) Your Daddy? Each generation has seen
the role of the father differently—from the pure breadwinners of the Silent and GI generations to the Dads of all Trades
(breadwinner, coach, cook, friend, hand-holder) we see now,
especially in Gen X. The result for fathers and their family businesses is confusion, conflict, and frustration, with
men in the business disagreeing about work-life balance and
Gen X dads feeling like they're falling short as professionals, fathers, husbands, and sons, with zero time for friends
and hobbies. All three George Browns in the opening case
contribute to this symptom, as George Sr. is all work, George
Jr. struggles with the father role, and George III feels caught
between work and home responsibilities, with almost zero
communication about the issue among the three.

Battle of the Super-Women. In Boomer and earlier generations, women forged strong careers by casting off gender ste-
reotypes and taking on more traditional male roles. Their
daughters, mostly Gen Xers, had an easier time climbing the
corporate ladder or finding a place in the family business—
often reporting to their moms or working alongside them.
Now, discrepant generation-based expectations about motherhood, management, and other topics cause these strong
women to clash, with negative implications for the business
and the family.

Meet the MEOWs—Mommy Executive Officer Women.
Gen X women today seem to have it all: strong careers,
family time, even some space for their own pursuits. So

why are many of them, especially leaders in family businesses, so unhappy? Just like their male counterparts suffering the symptom of Who's Your Daddy, Gen X women are cursed with too many choices: whether to focus on management, motherhood, makeovers, or all of the above, and many of them don't feel like they're succeeding in any of their roles. What's more, their moms, many of whom gave up or limited their own careers to stay at home, pressure them overtly or subtly to take on specific roles—the ones they themselves took on or left behind. Thirty-two-year-old Ellen Brown's challenges—balancing a busy work life, responsibilities at home, and a disapproving mom—typify this symptom.

Boomer Retirement Mirage. For Boomers, retirement is often a moving target, always just ahead but never at hand. At best, retirement is a mix of i-n-g's: golfing, gardening, sailing, reading, and, yes, working. And that means their Gen X children, now finding their own way as family business managers, have to deal with Mom and Dad whether they want to or not, which in turn means confusion and conflict over roles, responsibilities, and boundaries. George Brown Jr. struggles with this symptom, one that will likely have implications for the extended family in the near future.

My Child, My Boss. "If our roles were switched, I would do things differently," children often tell their parents. In many family businesses today, the roles *are* switched, with sons and daughters, Gen X and especially Gen Y, managing their parents—whether either side likes it or not. This is the flip-side of Boomer Retirement Mirage; in this case, frustration and conflict result from the seemingly impossible task of reconciling "I gave birth to you" with "I report to you."

Generation-Straddling Sibs. Longer spans between biological siblings and rising rates of blended families and half-siblings, especially among Boomers and Gen X and Y, have placed many brothers and sisters squarely in different generations. This phenomenon creates several challenges for siblings in family businesses, with expectations complicated by degree of relatedness and conflicting generation-based values, among others. George Jr. and the rest of the family face challenges dealing with Uncle Ben, partly because George Jr. and Ben are only half-siblings (and George Jr. feels Ben receives preferential treatment) and partly because Ben straddles Boomer and Gen X generations, with a hodgepodge of values from each (and of course partly because Ben thinks intense pink bellies are funny).

Overbalanced Gen X. Partly as a backlash to the workaholism of the 1980s and 1990s, many Gen Xers today, including family business owners and managers, have gone too far in the other direction, all in the name of work-life balance: focusing on family, fitness, and "finding themselves" to the point that their careers—along with the companies they work for—languish. And the problem's even more complicated when they work for Mom and Dad, who are always quick to remind them of what they themselves gave up to build the family business. George III and Ellen struggle with balance, and George III shows more signs of potential overbalance, which could result in greater conflict within the family down the line.

WimpY Gen Y. We've been called a "nation of wimps," with Gen Y bearing the brunt of this criticism. Regardless of what you call it, Generation Y, the newest to the workforce, does indeed have a problem. Too many of their "helicopter" parents did too much for them—in the sandbox, during all school years, even at their first jobs. Now they have to sort out their professional responsibilities and career paths, including within family businesses, but lack the tools and initiative. Worse, the same parents who helped create the problem often express puzzlement about their lack of initiative, and look to their Gen Y kids to solve things on their own—"you're an adult now"—especially in the context of family businesses.

This list of interrelated symptoms can certainly feel overwhelming for family business members. Luckily, we can approach the symptoms with a straightforward set of treatment steps.

Treating Stack-Up Symptoms

Like most syndromes, stack-up can be treated. That's what most of this book is about. I treat stack-up by first assessing the extent of the problem and its specific symptoms—including by using informal diagnostic criteria—then using education and specific exercises/treatments to help family businesses understand the problem patterns and diminish individual symptoms. While I can't prescribe Prozac, I do advise some of my families to consult a mental health professional. Seriously.

The next chapters of this book will outline various symptoms and scenarios within generational stack-up and how to recognize and address them. Each chapter presents a case example of a family business facing the featured stack-up symptom, followed by sections on how the symptom came to be (e.g., demographic trends related to it), diagnosing it, and the best treatment approach to it.

Here are the major steps I take to treat any symptoms of stack-up.

UNDERSTANDING THE PATTERNS→CHANGING THE PATTERNS→MAINTAINING THE CHANGES

Let's talk about each of these.

Understanding the Stack-Up Patterns

Assessing the problem. First I use extensive conversations with clients to understand the specific problems they face and their contributions to these as a group and as individuals. Family business clients come to me with all sorts of issues—succession, governance, share distribution—but underlying these are almost always jealousy, perceptions of injustice, or just plain dissatisfaction. Often these are rooted in longstanding patterns (even from childhood) among family members. And frequently the patterns have a lot to do with stack-up: the clash of discrepant values and expectations among members of different generations.

Regardless of the specific stack-up symptom or related problems a given family business is facing, a dialogue can be started around it—always the first step in treatment, after diagnosis—by answering some specific questions. I help them do that as a first step by asking questions. Among the key questions are:

- What are your biggest concerns for the business? For your family? For yourself? How do you feel you may have contributed to these?
- What frustrates you about the business/family situation, especially with regard to the actions/attitudes of other members?
- How do you think other members of your family (especially those working for the business) would answer the questions above (i.e., what are their biggest concerns)?

Each of the symptoms in the next chapters can first be approached by answering these and other questions, so refer back to this section when reading about specific symptoms. And family members need to answer the questions as honestly as possible, even if it's painful for them and others (and it likely will be). For many families, it's the first time they've discussed these, and they're often surprised to hear how much they have to say about them. When I spoke to the Brown family (they contacted me soon after the pink-belly incident), several conversations with individual members were hours-long. They'd been dissatisfied for a long time, but hadn't ever spoken about it in such an objective way.

Understanding the patterns. After this crucial assessment step, I focus more on education, laying out the stack-up–related patterns to help them understand how much specific generational differences contribute to their communication and other challenges. Sometimes I use symptom names to help them understand what they're up against. Sometimes I don't. I also use specific concepts (sometimes with visuals) to help them understand stack-up and its symptoms. I'll present these in the chapters on specific symptoms.

Overall, I view my role with clients largely as that of a "cross-generational translator." That is, I help each generation understand the others and ultimately speak the others' language—or, more realistically, reaching a point where they speak a shared language, one that uses terms and ideas from across generations.

As the Browns and I discussed stack-up and its symptoms, they expressed initial skepticism ("our problems are unique"), followed by deeper understanding. "It's like these symptoms were based on us," George III said in one meeting. He was right; I based the symptoms on families facing challenges just like theirs.

As part of this step, I help each member place their specific contributions to stack-up into context, emphasizing how it fits into the bigger picture of their challenges as a family. I link their struggles to generational differences and personality factors. For example, I helped George Jr. understand how his expectations of himself reflected typical Boomer struggles with dedication to work over other elements of life, and how these resulted in his personal "retirement mirage," along with how they fell squarely between George Sr.'s work-first mentality and George III's greater (though still challenging) flexibility. I also helped George III and his sister Ellen understand that their work-life balance issues were symptomatic of Gen Xers, and unlikely to be understood fully by members of previous generations, including their parents. I emphasize that family businesses may not be able to change certain generational influences, but that understanding them will help them see the big picture of their contributions to the family's challenges, and potentially alter negative patterns.

Changing the Patterns

In the next phase I help clients make real changes to the stack-up patterns they're caught in, often starting with smaller steps; it's important for them to understand they can't change everything at once. In general, the changes I recommend range from fostering communication among family members who tend to avoid each other to prioritizing "me-time" for certain individuals to helping others understand and change their damaging behavior. I recommend using regular family meetings with specific agendas and I help families think about how to start having fun together. In making recommendations, I typically use a structure to help me think about the specific ways a given family's problems show up. This might be based on inter- and intra-generational patterns or specific treatment steps. If I think it's helpful, I might share the structure I'm using with the family. The chapters on symptoms include several examples of these structures, but they can be used across symptoms, depending on what's best for your family.

I used several tactics to help the Browns. For example, it was clear that everyone was afraid to confront George Sr. about his control issues, especially given his declining health. I encouraged George Jr. and George III to understand that George Sr.'s behavior was typical of successful men in his generation, but also that they should sit down with the eldest Brown and explain, for the first time, that they wanted to be trusted with smaller tasks and not have George Sr. looking over their shoulders. I suggested they discuss how relinquishing some control would free George Sr. to focus on bigger-picture issues, including growth strategy and responses to new competitors. I guided them to present this to George Sr. as an "experiment" to improve efficiency, and cautioned that they shouldn't be surprised if George Sr. was resistant. After all, he'd been running Brown Industrials his way for over 60 years.

Similarly, I took the time to understand Ben's issues, given how central his behavior was to the family's challenges.

Though unwilling to express dissatisfaction at first ("We're a big messy family, just like any other"), Ben eventually discussed how difficult it had been to gain acceptance by the family—largely because he was only a half-sibling to George Jr. and, as a Boomer-Gen X cusper, "stuck" between George Jr.'s generation and that of George Jr.'s kids, leaving him unsure of how to relate to either. Ben explained how his joking around was part of his personality but also reflected his attempts to gain acceptance, and how his long trips were partly to avoid the disapproval he felt from the rest of the family. I helped Ben understand the generational influences on his behavior, and encouraged him to share some of his true feelings with the family, as a means of bridging the divide between them. I also asked him to work more collaboratively with Ellen, rather than making unreasonable last-minute requests, to help her balance her work and home responsibilities better—and to improve their relationship.

Though these and other steps were difficult for the Browns to take, once they started, they made progress quickly, with better communication and collaboration.

Maintaining the Change

To slip up is human. Inevitably, family businesses, even those who make fast and deep progress, have setbacks. It's no surprise, given that stack-up–related problems are often decades in the making. So I typically schedule check-ins approximately every six months, more frequently immediately after treatment.

Three months after I worked with the Browns, they'd maintained much of their progress: George Sr. had actually loosened his grip on some aspects of the company (e.g., new hires), allowing George Jr. and others to make decisions more on their own than ever. Both George III and Ellen reported improvement in their work-life balance; Ellen's progress was partly related to Uncle Ben's following through on his pledge to no longer dump work on her at the last minute. Perhaps not surprisingly, though, Ben had remained largely in his previous role—the joker who left on long trips and sometimes made everyone uncomfortable. "I tried to be serious, but they didn't take me seriously," Ben confided in me. I acknowledged the challenge Ben faced, but encouraged him to give it time. I also suggested that he didn't have to change his behavior 180 degrees; there were many benefits to his personality (e.g., clients appreciated his sense of humor), so the idea was to strike a balance between the "old Ben" and the "new Ben."

A year later, the Browns were on a much better path. George Sr. had delegated even more key responsibilities to family members and, seeing how well they handled these, begun talking about retirement—though everyone knew he would never remove himself entirely from the business he'd built. George Jr. enjoyed making more major decisions for Brown Industrials and, as George Sr.'s work-first attitude diminished, had taken more time for himself, including for painting classes. George III and Ellen continued to strive for work-life balance: George III had worked out a clearer schedule with his wife Judy (e.g., each week they selected one night, usually for one of Joey's events, that he wouldn't let work intrude on); Ellen arranged with Ben to work one day from home, allowing her to catch up on responsibilities there and spend more time with her daughter. Most remarkably, Ben had managed to achieve a great balance between old and new versions of himself. Still a jokester who enjoyed golf trips, he felt like he "belonged" in the family for the first time, largely because he'd learned to be more respectful of everyone else's preferences and time. "I realized I was pushing everyone away," he said, "then getting frustrated that no one appreciated me."

To celebrate their progress, the Browns even went on another Disneyworld trip. This time, they enjoyed a pleasant time at the pool, with Joey, Uncle Ben, and several others splashing in the water, no one's belly the slightest shade of pink.

Continuous Improvement, Not Fast Fixes

I've worked with hundreds of families like the Browns. Each of them has come to me in some kind of pain. Often they've tried to solve the problems they're facing themselves. Or they just hoped they'd go away. What I offer each family is a combination of encouragement, reassurance, information (especially about generational stack-up symptoms), and practical suggestions (ideally generated with the family) for managing and resolving their issues.

And ultimately "management" of the problem is what works, not one-time solutions. You have to take the long-term view. Stack-up and other core problems will continue to emerge in the form of different symptoms in multiple dimensions within the family and business. Recognizing the patterns and addressing the symptoms with the idea of making continuous improvement helps keep stack-up patterns from getting out of control.

So how do I know this approach works? Largely because clients tell me that it does, and they send other families to me to help them. But also because the families themselves see improvements over time—family branches that weren't speaking to each other now get together regularly; businesses on the brink of being sold off to divide the proceeds are now moving forward with a cohesive family management team; members who were scared to leave the business because they feared their relatives' reactions now have fulfilling careers outside the business, with their family's blessings.

Of course there are always situations that don't turn out as optimally. It's hard to say exactly why: sometimes they aren't ready to take on the problems; sometimes the stack-up–based approach doesn't seem to "click" with them. But most still feel they've learned something from the process.

In the next section of the book, we'll discuss nine symptoms of stack-up—what they look like, where they come from, and how to treat them. In each chapter, you'll meet a different family, come to know the problems and stack-up symptoms they're facing, and read about practical solutions to their issues. Each of these families, including the Browns, represents a *composite* of different families I've worked with. So the case examples—including names, details, quotes, and the like—are inspired by reality, rather than reflecting it exactly. Hopefully you can draw parallels between these families and your own, as you begin to understand and address the role generational stack-up plays in your family and business.

2

Control beyond the Grave

Members of the Silent and GI generations have been through a lot—an economic depression, several wars, and a decades-long booming global economy followed immediately by a major recession. On the one hand, this has resulted in a resilient, "can-do" cohort praised by many as "The Greatest Generation." On the other, the stress and uncertainty these groups have gone through creates mindsets that can cause conflict for them and those around them, including in family businesses. Business owners from these generations sometimes struggle to relinquish control, having nurtured the companies they founded for decades. Their clinging to control can stifle the growth of later generations, the very people expected to take the firm's reins. What's more, it's a pattern that tends to repeat itself from generation to generation. Thus addressing the generational stack-up dynamics reflected in this symptom is crucial to gaining control of it and achieving what all generations involved wish for: the healthy continuity of the business.

Some Decade, All This Will Be Yours

When Hank Sterling saw the red pickup truck pull onto the construction site in the late afternoon, his heart started pounding. Seeing his father's vehicle always had this effect on Hank, because the sight rarely meant anything good. Sure enough, when Doug Sterling stepped out of the truck, he was scowling. "Have you heard from Jimmy?" Doug yelled at his older son from across the site. Hank shook his head. It was true; he hadn't spoken to his younger brother that day. But it didn't really matter. Doug was frustrated about something, as always, and he would take it out on one or both sons, treating the men—who were nearing middle age—like they were still boys incapable of making good decisions, business-related or otherwise.

It was the start of a typical day for Sterling Transportation, a construction-supplies trucking company now in its third generation. Doug's father, Dennis, had started the company decades earlier, growing it from one truck to a whole fleet that hauled concrete, lumber, and other materials in several Midwestern states. Meticulous to a fault, Dennis had minded every detail of the growing company, from operations to credit to payroll, hiring managers in these areas but constantly looking over their shoulders, especially as the U.S. economy recovered from the Great Depression. When Doug joined the business immediately after high school he was no exception to Dennis's scrutiny. Doug, a natural with numbers, showed early talent for operations and negotiations, wringing greater and greater efficiency from the routes and negotiating better terms with key customers. But Dennis questioned him at every step, making his son go over the business cases repeatedly and often reversing Doug's decisions, even as Doug rose to taking charge of operations. Occasionally, after an especially good week, Dennis would pat his son on the shoulder and say, "Someday, all this will be yours."

Not surprisingly, that day came nearly two decades after Doug had expected it—when his father became bedridden in his late 80s. Doug immediately took advantage of his new leadership role, making operational improvements (e.g., a new information management system) Dennis had resisted for years. He also dove into other areas of the business, meeting frequently with managers of all divisions. Armed with the bigger-picture knowledge he gained, Doug developed even more effective operational and business development strategies, helping Sterling Transportation rise quickly to a major industry player in the Midwest. The downside to his success was that he had forged it just as his father Dennis had: by maintaining tight control over every function of the business.

Fast forward 20 years, to the day the appearance of Doug's red pickup on a customer's construction site made his son Hank cringe. By then, Doug was 73. Hank, the older son, was 44, and Jimmy was 38. According to his business cards, Hank was VP of Business Development, a natural role for him, given his easygoing nature and people skills. In fact, many key customer contacts had confided in Hank that they preferred dealing with him alone, but that wasn't really an option; Doug came to every major meeting. In fact, when the senior Sterling was running late, Hank knew better than to start the meeting without him, even if that meant waiting hours. And while Hank had proposed some innovative ideas soon after joining the business, including using higher-tech customer management tools, he'd learned that Doug had little interest in such improvements. "One bad decision could mean the end," his father always said.

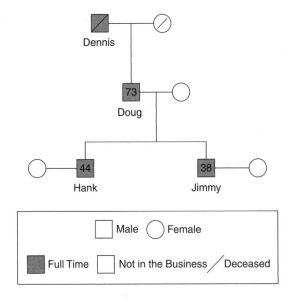

Figure 2.1   Control beyond the Grave: The Sterling Family

Younger son Jimmy shared his father's facility with numbers, so Doug had groomed him for an operations role starting with summer internships in college (both boys had attended college at Doug's urging, but their father frequently reminded them that he had a "degree in experience"). But Jimmy quickly found that Doug couldn't really trust an analysis unless he himself had done it. "Let me take a better look at this," Doug would say when Jimmy presented a spreadsheet for improved routing or other aspects of operations. Inevitably Doug would implement "Jimmy's plan" with completely reworked numbers. For years Jimmy had hoped his father would learn to trust him more, believing that it was merely a matter of time or his presenting better analyses. When it became clear that Doug wasn't going to change, Jimmy—by then heading operations, the role his father had once had—gave up. Robbed of confidence and belief in his value to the business, he spent most of his time doing "research" in the field, driving the routes their trucks followed, taking long breaks along the way.

In fact, the afternoon Doug was looking for Jimmy (for some routing information Jimmy had), his younger son was miles away, sitting in a roadside bar and grill, his cell phone turned off. "Can't rely on that boy for anything," Doug said to Hank on the construction site. Briefly, Hank thought to contradict his father—he knew Jimmy was capable, and he told his younger brother that routinely, the many times they commiserated over a beer about Doug's controlling nature. But Hank knew that saying anything about it to Doug would only bring their father's wrath on himself. So he nodded, hoping that would be the end of it. Hank called it "staying out of Dad's trouble spot," and it was a game both sons played. Short of blaming each other when things went wrong, the brothers would just agree with their father about everything, including his dissatisfaction with each of them.

On a more practical level, Doug's management style caused almost daily headaches. The biggest issue was his tendency to pull resources out from under his sons and other managers on a whim. If Hank had to line up three trucks for a long haul for a new customer, he would commit six vehicles, because he knew Doug might grab any that he needed at the last minute—and not even tell Hank about it. The situation left employees caught in the middle repeatedly, but in the end they always knew whose orders took precedence: Doug's.

All of the challenges Sterling Transportation faced took place in a very difficult business environment, one growing bleaker with each new gloomy headline. After enjoying two decades of disproportionate growth driven by rising U.S. real estate prices, the building industry was in steep decline, and players in every sub-sector, including transportation, were folding or being purchased at bargain-basement prices. Either option—closing or selling—meant "defeat" to Doug. Fortunately, Sterling was still profitable, but the bottom line was falling fast as customers canceled large contracts and demanded lower pricing. And though they never shared it with their father, both Hank and Jimmy believed that selling might not be a bad thing—two larger, national-level players had made offers for Sterling that Doug had dismissed—in part because of the financial aspect and in part because it would relieve the stress of dealing with their father. Hank and Jimmy knew Doug wouldn't be willing to sell the business, but they had no idea what his plan for succession or ownership was, and they knew better than to ask their father about it.

The stress of the situation spilled over to each Sterling household and the relationships among them. The three families spent time together—Saturdays at the youngest generation's baseball and basketball games, Sunday barbecues at the two-acre spread Doug had inherited from Dennis, and other get-togethers. But the family time was increasingly tense: everyone knew the challenges of the economy and, unlike the brothers themselves, Hank and Jimmy's wives were willing to speak up about some of the family dynamics, blaming Doug and the other sibling for standing in their husbands' way. Earlier in the year, at a family dinner in a restaurant, the two women had gotten into a big argument about the situation, and had only recently been on speaking terms again. Hank and Jimmy tended to stay out of such fights, given how many challenges they were already managing at work.

There were rare moments when Hank and Jimmy felt more positive about the present and future. Sometimes, especially after a week of better returns from the business, Doug would sit down with his sons at the main office and sweep a hand around the room. "Someday, boys," he would say, echoing his own father, "all of this will be yours." Hank and Jimmy appreciated the sentiment, but couldn't help wondering how long it might be before that "someday" arrived, and what exactly would be left of the "all this" by then.

Control beyond the Grave: The Symptom

None of the Sterlings realized it, but they were caught in a symptom of generational stack-up that they didn't even start. They inherited the frustration-causing dynamics from Dennis, Doug's father and the founder of Sterling Transportation. By taking an overly controlling approach to the business and second-guessing Doug on everything he did, Dennis prevented Doug from gaining key management skills, including trusting in his own judgment and delegating key tasks to others. As a result, when Doug finally inherited leadership of the business, he did exactly what his father had done: he tried to do everything himself, effectively handcuffing his sons and other managers, resulting in a lot of frustration and, presumably, poorer business performance.

We can think of the symptom as generally related to "Founder's Syndrome," or the tendency for the founder of a business to overstay his or her period of most effective management and to maintain too much control over decision making as the organization grows in size, scope, and sophistication. Founder's Syndrome has been recognized as an issue in businesses and other organizations ever since individuals started launching these.[1] But Control beyond the Grave has become even farther-reaching in recent years for one simple reason: we're living longer and better than ever.

Longer Lives and Generational Clashes

As discussed in Chapter 1, life expectancy in industrialized nations has risen dramatically in recent decades. Since 1950, lifespan has risen nearly 30 years in the United States,[2] and one of the country's fastest-growing groups is individuals over 100 years old.[3] Our longer, healthier lifespan, which underlies the syndrome of generational stack up in general, means that each generation of a family business is able to maintain control of the business for much longer than in the past. And that's not always a good thing, as the Sterling example suggests. For example, succession issues in earlier times (for businesses, kingdoms, and other hierarchical organizations) essentially "took care of themselves," as founders and their immediate successors generally didn't enjoy the longevity and quality of life to maintain control over the organization for decades. Today, they do.

Fast Fact

There may be 1 million centenarians (individuals 100 years or older) in the United States by the year 2050.

Source: Based on growth rates for this demographic; "Geographical Factors Influencing Living to 100" (http://www.thecentenarian. co.uk/geographical-factors-influencing-living-to-one-hundred. html) (accessed April 16, 2010).

But longer lifespans aren't the only driver of Control beyond the Grave. Generational differences play a clear role as well. One of the most obvious complicating factors in the Sterling Transportation example is Doug's unwillingness to share control of the business, something he "inherited" from his own father. Taking leadership of the business later in life than ideal (some of his peers had taken top management roles in their family businesses 20 years before he did) contributed to Doug's controlling nature, as did the context in which he was raised. As a Silent Generation member, Doug was a child of the Depression, and he took a very careful approach to risk; as his own father had reminded him after he joined the business, "one bad decision" could end it all.

Moreover, Doug's attitude and risk aversion conflicted with his sons' approach, in part because both younger men are part of Generation X, a group that as a whole takes a more entrepreneurial, risk-seeking approach and embraces a greater focus on family than previous generations. This is on top of the predictable difference in risk aversion between older and younger people, with the latter generally willing to take on more risk. The generational influences were reflected in several areas. First, Doug's unilateral dismissal of Hank's ideas for business improvements highlighted the difference in risk profiles between the generations and led Hank eventually to stop trying. Second, Jimmy's willingness to "check out" of his business responsibilities quickly and avoid dealing with the situation more directly might be viewed as symptomatic of his generation: witnessing the crumbling of longstanding institutions like the nuclear family and the typical corporate job made this cohort more skeptical than their predecessors, and thus more willing to give up on conventional ideals. Finally, the conflict among members of the extended Sterling family reflects Generation–X–related patterns as well. In earlier generations, spouses rarely would have become as openly involved in business-related issues as Hank and Jimmy's wives were. But Gen X has a sharp focus on work-life balance, which includes blurrier lines between business and family, and thus allows for more clashes of this sort.

Finally, beyond longer lifespans and generational influences, there was a third clear factor in the Sterling Transportation example: the declining economy. In 2008 the United States entered an economic recession driven largely by a rapid drop in artificially elevated real estate prices and a related stagnant credit market. The "fat and happy" years that preceded this decline had eroded many good habits of management and ownership, as businesses traded fundamentals-driven discipline for the belief that rapid short-term growth would never end. Instead, the rate of job loss in the following years was the worst since the 1940s,[4] and U.S. unemployment marched quickly to nearly 10 percent. This swift and far-reaching economic decline caused the family significant stress and worsened ongoing conflicts, including those related to the symptom of Control beyond the Grave.

So how can you tell if Control beyond the Grave is a real symptom in your family business?

Diagnosing Control beyond the Grave

The list below can help you think about whether your family business has issues related to Control beyond the Grave.

IF YOU AGREE MORE THAN DISAGREE WITH THESE STATEMENTS, CONTROL BEYOND THE GRAVE MAY BE A SYMPTOM WORTH TREATING IN YOUR FAMILY BUSINESS.

- In our business, the founder or oldest generation member tends to make all major decisions, even if the later generations have official leadership roles.
- Family and nonfamily employees in the business adhere to the wishes of the founding/older generation, even when that means going directly against the younger generation's requests or plans.
- The younger generation is dissatisfied with their leadership roles (i.e., titles and/or responsibilities) in the business and the time frame for their taking on greater leadership.
- There is a general lack of trust across generations for handling business and family issues.
- Younger-generation members don't feel that their opinions are heard and respected.
- Members of the extended family (including spouses and those not working in the' business) express frustration about the lack of leadership roles for the younger generation and a clear succession plan.
- The estate plan for the business is not shared and/or incomplete.

Control beyond the Grave: The Treatment

Families must first understand the generation-based patterns they've fallen into and why. Then practical steps are developed to alter these patterns.

Understanding the Stack-Up Patterns

After considering a series of questions about their situation (see Chapter 1), families can begin to understand their specific issues within a context, linking their challenges to underlying sources. For the Sterlings, this meant highlighting the roles that demographic patterns, generational influences, and the economy have played (as reflected in the *Longer Lives and Generational Clashes* section above). I explained how the fact that we're all living longer is both a good and a bad thing for family businesses: it means that founders can enjoy healthy involvement with the business much longer than in the past, but also that there will be much more tension around leadership roles and succession. I also pointed out how the "waiting game" that results is likely to repeat itself with each generation, as it had in their case. Doug admitted that he had never seen his deep involvement in the business as similar to his own father's; he thought of it just as evidence that he wanted what was "best" for the company.

Similarly, the three Sterling men were unaware of the strong generation-based influences in their situation. Hank and Jimmy merely saw their father as "scared" of big changes and "stubborn" about the idea of selling, rather than understanding how these were natural consequences of growing up in the shadow of the Depression. In the same way, I tried to get Doug to understand that his sons' greater flexibility with business matters and willingness to involve their spouses in these were typical of members of their generation, rather than reflecting their idiosyncrasies or general opposition to him. We all agreed that the economic decline wasn't helping matters, and I urged them to view it as a challenge they could face together, rather than one that would split them further apart.

Throughout, I emphasized that the process we were going through wasn't about forcing individuals to change into something they weren't comfortable with, but to help them understand how to work better together. Armed with this idea and a deeper understanding of the factors contributing to the situation, we moved on into changing the patterns, which in this case meant addressing several sets of issues within the business and family.

Changing the Stack-Up Patterns

The Sterlings had to address three specific areas to improve their family relationships and business performance.

Intergenerational issues. In many ways, this set of dynamics was the most prominent for the Sterlings, as Doug failed to put sufficient trust in his sons and they, in turn, stopped having much active involvement in the business. While understanding some of the factors (e.g., those that were generation-based) that had led to the current situation was helpful for the three of them, I made clear that it wasn't enough to drive long-lasting improvements, and urged them to take several practical steps.

The big theme of the practical steps was communication. Rather than avoiding their father or whispering behind his back about the challenges they faced with him, Hank and Jimmy had to begin speaking with "one voice" to Doug, and it had to be an audible one. Initially, this meant being more vocal about day-to-day issues that came up, including Doug's tradition of "stealing" resources out from under his sons. I suggested they develop a daily operations schedule that each of the three would sign off on, and then hold one another to it, with token penalties (e.g., a nominal dollar amount) for deviating from it.

To build on the idea of communication, I asked them to institute regular meetings (1) among the three of them, and (2) between Doug and each son, to discuss big-picture and more routine business matters. The three-way meeting would help Hank and Jimmy speak with one voice to their father (and eventually raise major issues including succession), while the two-person meetings would help each son tackle specific issues with Doug, such as Hank's ideas for tech-based customer relationship management and Jimmy's operations analyses. Not surprisingly, the three Sterlings were initially reluctant about having such regular contact—they had become comfortable with their avoidance of one another—but they agreed to try. Along with focusing on business-related communication, I recommended that the three men make much more of an effort to spend time together on fun activities. Not surprisingly, as tensions rose in the office over the years, Doug and his sons had stopped spending almost any free time together. For example, they had enjoyed deep-sea fishing together when the boys were growing up, and had even talked about taking another trip sometime, but hadn't for years. I suggested it was time to dust off their rods and reels.

Naturally it was slow going at first, but in the months that followed, Doug, Hank, and Jimmy began communicating more effectively, and working better together as a result. They also managed to take a long overdue fishing trip.

Intragenerational issues. While it appeared that Hank and Jimmy were supportive of each other, and in many ways they were, their interaction was also part of the problem. Specifically, by being careful not to disagree with Doug when he expressed dissatisfaction with the other sibling, each of the sons was undermining the other. Recall that both sons generally sought to avoid Doug's "trouble spot," even if that meant siding with their father against the other—sometimes merely by agreeing with him. That behavior played right into a pattern that psychologists call "triangulation," or the use of a third party by two people to avoid issues between them. Hank and Jimmy had to give this pattern a hard look, and to call each other on it when they saw it happening, with the goal of eventually replacing it with a healthier response. "So what do we say when Dad starts complaining about one of us to the other?" they asked. "For starters you could tell him that that's between him and your brother," I said. It was a simple policy, but an important one that would help the family move from triangulation to "straight-line" relationships.

Extended-family issues. Families fight. It's part and parcel of dealing with the same set of people for decades, often in close quarters and often with very long memories of specific insults or injustices. But business families are prone to particularly nasty battles, as issues including ownership and succession frequently enter the picture. The Sterlings were no exception; observing their husbands' frustration with leadership and other issues, Hank and Jimmy's wives had taken up the cause, even to the point of arguing with each other about it. Initially, Hank and Jimmy claimed they had "nothing to do" with the issue, and that their wives had "minds of their own." I encouraged them to see their role in the dynamic—by complaining about the situation at work but doing little to address it, they were tacitly encouraging their wives to get involved, then distancing themselves from the whole thing. In essence, every adult member of the extended Sterling family was playing "the blame game," assigning responsibility for their own troubles to others.

Again, a communication breakdown is almost always at the heart of such matters. To address it, they needed regular family meetings—including spouses—to discuss issues as they came up, rather than letting these spill over to what should have been enjoyable events, such as dinners out. The early family meetings should lay out the "ground rules" for subsequent meetings (e.g., types of issues open for discussion). Also, some part of the meeting time should be reserved for planning fun activities for the extended family.

A frequent underlying issue with a family like the Sterlings is that they have very limited organizational experience, individually and collectively. The family business is their only reference point. That was certainly the case here, as Doug, Hank, and Jimmy had only worked in the family firm. So they had to develop basic organizational and communication skills to use with one another, the broader business, and their partners and customers. Often families say this "feels too corporate," so it's important for them to understand the benefits of a more professional approach and find ways to incorporate this into their own business.

The Sterlings reported that they "didn't say much" in the first two meetings they planned, but that by the third, they'd begun to raise important issues including leadership roles and how best to cope with the challenging economic times. Given a "safe" place to discuss business and family issues, Hank and Jimmy's wives had also been enjoying a much more amicable relationship. It's important for the family to think of the process as similar to learning to ride a bike. There will be falls, short rides that end unexpectedly, and bone-jarring crashes, and many times it will be difficult to recognize progress. But success comes with dedication and practice; you learn to keep your balance and then you learn to use more sophisticated strategies (e.g., using the brakes rather than stopping by falling). It's also critical to focus on fundamentals and details, especially as you take on more challenging goals; the most successful business families are analogous to Tour de France champion teams, always looking to hone their skills and work better together.

Maintaining Changes

The patterns families have to deal with have taken years, often decades, to form. That's especially true with the symptom of Control beyond the Grave, which almost always starts with the founding generation. Given how deeply rooted the patterns are, it's important to remember that they can't be dismissed overnight.

That was certainly the case with the Sterlings. The good news was that they were communicating much better—Doug, Hank, and Jimmy had kept their promise to one another of meeting regularly to talk through issues and ideas. The benefits were clear: both Hank and Jimmy felt that their voices were being heard better by Doug than before, and both had stepped up their involvement in the business in general. Jimmy and Hank had also done a good job of supporting each other by forcing Doug to deal with them directly, rather than playing into the same old pattern of triangulation. The family reported that the spouses continued to get along better as well.

At the same time some of the previous issues remained. While Doug met with his sons regularly, he still had trouble relinquishing control of major areas. For example, while Doug listened more carefully to Jimmy's ideas for operational improvements, he was still reluctant to implement any changes without running all the numbers himself, which continued to frustrate his younger son. Similarly, though the economy continued to decline, Doug dismissed any interest from buyers out of hand, to his sons' dismay.

Two things exhibited just how much progress they'd made: (1) for the first time Doug had started talking about his estate plan, even asking his sons for their input, and (2) Hank and Jimmy both said that they no longer cringed whenever they saw their father's red pickup truck approaching.

3

Who's (or What's) Your Daddy?

Today's dads come in many shapes and sizes; many of us are still the primary breadwinner in the family, but most of us place much greater emphasis on family than our counterparts in previous generations, including our own fathers. On the one hand, that represents progress from a time not so long ago when men rose early each day, went to work, then came home and focused as much or more on a cocktail and the newspaper than on their children. On the other hand, today's men, especially Gen Xers, are faced with daily dilemmas around choosing work, family, or their own pursuits. And it's even more complicated in family businesses where men from different generations work together, each bringing biases and expectations about work-life balance. This chapter helps fathers, sons, and those around them deal with the frustration this tricky situation often generates.

Tom Walker's Tough Choices

"You needed to keep your eye on the ball and swing through with your hips."

That's what 42-year-old Tom Walker imagined his father saying after senior management and board meetings, even though the events had nothing to do with baseball, and even if Tom, vice president of sales at U.S. Lawn and Lumber (USLL), a multimillion-dollar regional player, had performed very well in the meeting. Those were the kinds of things Tom's dad, Robert, said after watching Tom's baseball games years ago—the rare times Robert attended a game. Now 72, Robert was still going strong as USLL's CEO. And he looked every bit the part: a tall, broad-shouldered man with the requisite booming voice. When Robert entered a room, he commanded immediate respect. And, in many ways, the older Walker still terrified his son Tom.

It's not that Tom was incompetent or even mediocre as a manager. In fact, he was a very well-respected executive and great communicator who worked his way up over 15 years: from salesperson to sales manager to general manager to his current executive role. Tom was the clear frontrunner to succeed his father as CEO in the near future. Yet his anxiety stemmed from his memories of how absent and hard-to-please his father had been when he was a child, and his father's ongoing—though generally unvoiced—disapproval of Tom's willingness to sacrifice work for family.

When Tom, the oldest of three siblings, was a boy, his father, the founder of USLL, was busy building the family business, which naturally took him away from the family. Given Tom's success with sports—he excelled in baseball, basketball, and golf—there were many events for Robert to miss. "I think he made one or two games a season," Tom said, recalling his disappointment when his father had to miss a regional basketball championship for a last-minute client meeting. Not that Robert's rare appearances were all that welcome. Rather than praise for his son's performance or consolation about errors or losses, Robert typically offered blunt advice about everything from batting and passing skills to conditioning and teamwork. Not surprisingly, Tom often performed worse at the few games Robert attended.

Home life wasn't much different. Robert made family dinners a priority despite his busy schedule, but as hard as the Walker children and Lucy, their mother, tried to have a pleasant meal, the children often found themselves in polite arguments at best and tearful confrontations at worst with Robert over a wide spectrum of topics: high school and college courses, personal finance management, politics, even whom they were dating. Light conversations were rare. In retrospect, all three siblings had no recollection of a single instance of praise or other positive feedback from their father. Their mother, Lucy, was more nurturing, but she was naturally reluctant to cross Robert, and spent much of her time attending business-related social and community events, flawlessly playing the role of a supportive, at-home spouse through the 1960s, 70s, and 80s.

At college and beyond, the Walker children continued to anticipate with anxiety their father's reactions and opinions about their choices. The family gathered frequently, but as Tom recalled, the get-togethers were marked by "awkwardness and tension" as the siblings and their mother treaded carefully through one conversational minefield after another. USLL was growing quickly, and the family was enjoying an even higher standard of living, with a larger house in an upscale neighborhood, nicer cars, and frequent vacations. But overworked Robert had become even harder to please.

After college, despite Robert's protests, Tom pursued professional golf, teaching the sport at a country club and tending bar to pay the bills. After two years, when it became clear that Tom couldn't make the professional circuit, he reluctantly joined USLL. "I liked the industry and in some ways it seemed like what I was meant to do," Tom recalled. Around the same time he married Jody, his college sweetheart; soon after, the couple had their first of three children. Even before he became a father, Tom had made a rock-solid resolution: "I wasn't going to be like my dad." He planned to build a successful career while devoting ample time—and nurturance—to his family, especially his children. "I aimed to be at every game," Tom said.

Yet Tom quickly discovered the challenges of living out his resolution. Like Tom's mother, his wife, Jody, chose to stay at home soon after having their first child; USLL's ongoing success and generous compensation allowed the couple to make

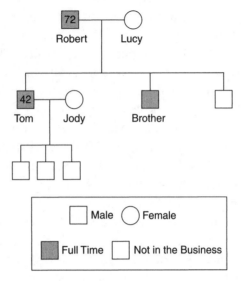

Figure 3.1   Who's (or What's) Your Daddy? The Walker Family

this decision more easily. But unlike Lucy, Jody expected Tom to be much more involved with the children—in part because he'd expressed a strong desire to do this—even though she was home full-time. Also unlike Lucy, Jody wasn't willing to constrain her role to that of "company spouse"; she had an active social life and often needed Tom to cover her for evenings or entire weekends. The situation required Tom to make tough choices almost daily: Should he miss a key sales meeting to attend a T-ball game? Should he give up a planned golf outing to stay home with the kids while Jody enjoyed a last-minute "girls' weekend" in Las Vegas? Should he rush out of work early on a weekday to attend an important parent-teacher meeting? As he struggled with these decisions, Tom felt that he wasn't measuring up to his standards for any of the roles he held: he was always behind at work and delegating too many tasks to his managers; he was spending more time than his father had with his children but always felt distracted by what he was missing or behind on at work; he and Jody bickered frequently about his work schedule and level of distraction; he never saw his few remaining friends.

"I'm going nonstop but don't feel like I'm getting anywhere," he said.

What's more, Tom knew that his father disapproved of his choices. Early on Robert said little directly, but often gave his son looks that communicated loud and clear: "Leaving early again?" his raised eyebrows said; "Who wears the pants in your family, son?" his frown said. Because Tom sensed Robert's disapproval, he tended to avoid the topic of work-life balance, typically sending Robert e-mails about upcoming responsibilities at home, rather than telling him directly. Tom figured Robert was unlikely to read the e-mails and, sure enough, his father rarely responded to them.

To make matters worse, Robert reserved his negativity for Tom, taking a surprisingly laid-back approach to Tom's younger brother, who had also joined the business by then. In fact, after Tom's brother made a major accounting error that Tom had to work several overnights to fix, Robert offered no praise, hardly even acknowledging the effort. The next day, when Tom was rushing to leave work for his son's baseball game, Robert passed him in the hall and said, "Where you going this time?" Tom struggled not to confront his father, to scream at him for all that he had missed when Tom was a child and to plead with him for the positive feedback Tom had needed so badly his entire life. Instead, Tom closed the door to his office and laid his head on his desk.

It was like he was 12 years old again, only worse: he felt like a failure as a son, professional, father, husband, and friend.

Who's Your Daddy: The Symptom

Tom Walker is not alone. Too many fathers worldwide, especially in the Western world, feel just like he does: they're not meeting their expectations of themselves in virtually all the roles they hold. They're perpetually behind at work, distracted when with their families, and scrambling to find any time for friends and hobbies.

They have no solutions.

The problem is likely worse for fathers working in family businesses, because they have the illusion of greater control over their schedules and responsibilities, especially if they're CEOs or executives. Like Tom, they may report to family members—often their own fathers—and hope that means greater understanding and accommodation of the tough choices they face. As Tom discovered, it often means the opposite.

The symptom of Who's Your Daddy, then, is reflected mainly in two phenomena: (1) the challenges and frustrations working fathers in current managerial roles (typically late Boomers or Gen Xers) face as they try to balance successful careers with deeply involved family lives and time for other personal pursuits, and (2) clashes between these men and their fathers (often their managers) as they attempt to strike this balance while the older generation may not even recognize the challenges their sons face. Tom and Robert Walker form a textbook example of this symptom: the younger Walker struggles to manage work and family responsibilities, leaving no time for friends or personal activities, all while facing the clear disapproval of his father. Neither feels understood or respected by the other.

Why do so many of today's working fathers, especially in family businesses, face these challenges? Because the long-established role of the father has changed dramatically in recent years. Let's take a look at the trends underlying this symptom.

Fathers Then and Now

Hunters, warriors, protectors, breadwinners.

For thousands of years and in almost every culture, these have been the roles a father is expected to play. "Nurturer" is not on that list. And "at-home" has only recently become an acceptable prefix to "dad." But "disciplinarian" has been another common role—making it no surprise that for decades children in the United States and elsewhere have lived in fear of the phrase "Wait until your father gets home!"

That's not to say that biology, or "hardwiring," doesn't play a part in the roles fathers and mothers gravitate toward.[1] But the social, cultural, economic and ideological constructs that prevail at the time are arguably more powerful influences on these roles and expectations.[2] These constructs have converged around the roles above, more or less, for millennia.

Until now.

Though there have been subtle and not-so-subtle shifts in father and mother roles in the last few centuries (e.g., greater division of labor between work and home brought on by industrialization in the nineteenth century[3]), the most dramatic changes have arrived only in the last 50 years—well into the lifetimes of most people reading this book. What these changes have meant is that fathers—and mothers—today effectively have many, many more choices than they did in the past around career, marriage, parenthood, geography, friendships, hobbies, and other areas. The definition of "acceptable" choices and behaviors has expanded dramatically. As fathers, we can choose to stay at home (if we're financially independent or our spouses earn enough), use unprecedented job flexibility to spend more time with our families (if we can make the finances work out), or step into the traditional working-dad role (if we opt for that as a couple). That's great, right?

Not always.

An abundance of choice has its downsides, as Tom Walker discovered firsthand. In fact, there's growing recognition that having too many choices, especially in important areas like finances, healthcare, and parental roles, is associated with a host of negative physical and psychological symptoms.[4] And there's another, more subtle factor at play: the expectation that working fathers not only *want* to spend more time with their families but *will*, regardless of how demanding their work is. This expectation, along with today's choice-rich context for dads and Tom's negative experiences as a child, prompted him to try to do it all: succeed as a rising family business executive, deeply involved father, and devoted husband. Instead he felt inadequate on all counts, in no small part because his own father failed to acknowledge or even understand the challenges Tom faced.

Robert, from the Silent Generation, and his Gen X son, Tom, were practically destined to butt heads or at least fail to understand each other with regard to their roles as fathers. The Silent Generation's prototypical father was the stable, hard-working breadwinner. Having grown up amidst the poverty and despair of the Great Depression that started in 1929, these men knew severe deprivation firsthand—of food, money, and happiness. As a result, they were "programmed" to keep their heads down and their noses to the proverbial grindstone, to avoid having to live with so little again. Like many men of his generation then, Robert had the "luxury" of fewer choices and an almost exclusive focus on hard work. Naturally, his son's struggles to balance work and homelife were foreign to him, and often sources of annoyance and disapproval. Tom, on the other hand, had trouble placing himself in Robert's shoes—in part because Robert spoke little of his own childhood—and thus blamed the elder Walker's hardness on his personality, rather than his early experiences. The understanding gap between the two was large and virtually impossible to cross.

Fast Fact

In 1965, only 5 percent of fathers witnessed their babies' births. In 2009, 95 percent did.

Source: Published on Pregnancy.org (http://www.pregnancy.org) Home > Men and Fatherhood: Pregnancy and Birth by Bruce Linton, Ph.D.

So the effects of the Who's Your Daddy symptom of generational stack-up are clear in Tom Walker's case. But how severe is this symptom in your family business?

Diagnosing Who's Your Daddy

IF YOU AGREE MORE THAN DISAGREE WITH THESE STATEMENTS, "WHO'S YOUR DADDY" MAY BE A

SYMPTOM WORTH TREATING IN YOUR FAMILY BUSINESS.

- Some fathers in our business struggle constantly to balance time with their children and time on the job.
- Fathers in our business disagree frequently about how to balance work and life.
- Some fathers in our business feel very guilty leaving the business to attend family events.
- Some fathers in our business feel very guilty being at work when their children have events or functions.
- Some fathers in our business are uncertain about expected role and contributions around the home beyond child-rearing activities.
- Some fathers in our business often disagree with their spouses about their expected role at home.
- Some fathers in our business spend little or no time on personal hobbies or with friends.

Who's Your Daddy: The Treatment

Families must first understand the generation-based patterns they've fallen into and why. Then practical steps are developed to alter these patterns.

Understanding the Stack-Up Patterns

After considering a series of questions about their situation (see Chapter 1), families can begin to understand their specific issues within a context, linking their challenges to underlying sources. For example, Tom understood the counterintuitive challenges of having too many choices and how his father's silence and single-minded focus on work was associated with the time in which Robert grew up. Through this process, which wasn't easy, Robert, and especially Tom, came to a greater understanding of their roles, the factors influencing their roles, and how their roles and expectations naturally clashed at times. This prepared them for the next step: changing the patterns.

Changing the Stack-Up Patterns

There are several practical steps that the Walkers could take to approach the symptom of Who's Your Daddy.

Improve communication. As a direct result of stack up, Tom and Robert had fallen into a highly dysfunctional and ineffective communication pattern—Tom avoided being direct with his father and Robert offered too many snide comments and too little encouragement. Recognizing that Tom was more likely to change his behavior than Robert, given his younger age and generation, Tom had to take a more direct communication approach with his father: rather than sending e-mails or avoiding the topic of his absences completely, he was to discuss each instance face-to-face. "Your dad will see you as a more capable businessperson this way," I told Tom, and asked him to promise to try the direct approach for three weeks; in that period he wasn't "allowed" to send e-mails about upcoming absences to Robert. Instead, he met briefly with his father to specify days or periods he would be out—and, at least as important, his plan for getting key projects done. The new communication pattern was foreign to both Walkers at first, and Tom was tempted to return to e-mailing after the first attempts. But, within a month, face-to-face communication on this topic became the norm. Tom found that preparing for the discussions actually helped him put together more efficient plans to get his work done and still spend time with his family, which helped him stay less distracted. As a bonus, Tom even received some of the positive feedback he wanted from Robert when his dad told him he was "getting things done well." Little wins mean a lot.

Prioritize "me-time." The last things Tom thought he had time for were his friends and hobbies, which included woodworking and golf. It was necessary for Tom to understand that, paradoxically, spending more time on himself would make him more effective in all of his roles. Making this happen was more of a challenge, given the family system Tom had helped create—a father who wanted him to work harder, a wife and kids who wanted him at home more and less distracted, and his own expectations that he should be everywhere and fully engaged at all times. Tom and Jody also had to determine a way to set new expectations; for the first time Tom shared his feelings of failure with his wife, and helped her understand how she could help. Jody, who wasn't from a family business herself, saw Tom's struggles in better context, and she encouraged him to take more time for himself. Together they also decided that Tom would stay late at the office one night a week, even if it meant missing family events, to stay on top of his growing responsibilities. As with the new communication pattern, Tom struggled at first to make these changes. But over time he settled into a healthier work-life balance that included working harder at times (e.g., one late night a week) and spending more time on himself without feeling guilty.

Set realistic expectations. Underlying many of the Walkers' challenges and frustrations was a mismatch in expectations. This was especially the case in the relationship between Tom and his father and between Tom and his wife, Jody. For example, Robert expected that Tom would prioritize work over everything else, as the elder Walker had done; Tom, in contrast, expected that his father would understand the work-life balance struggle Tom faced daily. Both Tom and Jody expected that each would understand the other's need for time for their own activities, including hobbies and spending time with friends. None of these expectations was being fulfilled, leading to a lot of tension and heartache and ultimately a *lack* of expectation of anything positive. Families like the Walkers have to break this pattern of mismatched expectations through a combination of communication and empathy. The Walkers had to first lay out expectations more clearly—partly by communicating more effectively, as discussed above—and then modify their expectations to be realistic. For example, it wasn't reasonable for Robert to expect Tom to be "just like Dad," nor was it reasonable for Tom to expect his father to think like a Gen Xer—the two Walkers were able to understand this by talking through (i.e., the communication part) their underlying expectations for the first time. After several weeks they were able to at least articulate what the other might expect of them (i.e., the empathy part), but also recognize that they couldn't always deliver this, given their personality, habits, and generational membership. Similarly, Tom and Jody became much more effective at checking with one another about the time they needed for their personal activities, and developed more realistic expectations about what was reasonable to ask for (e.g., Jody avoided scheduling more than one activity for herself on a given weekend). These more realistic expectations helped the family members balance their needs better with one another.

Maintaining Changes

Six months after working with Tom and Robert, I found that some of the old behaviors had returned. Tom was occasionally avoiding talking to his father directly about upcoming absences. He was also giving less priority to his own activities, often using the time he'd set aside to catch up on work or spend time with family. And father and son had missed some bonding events due to work commitments. They resolved to try harder.

After another six months had gone by, Tom was flying high. Though he'd taken on even more responsibilities at work, he felt he was performing better than ever. He'd also been much more engaged with his family, in part because he was using his weekly late night to catch up on key projects at work. "Just knowing I have that time helps me relax at home," he said. Tom was also golfing and enjoying woodworking regularly, using the former to reconnect with several old friends.

While Robert was still pretty much the same, and was never going to become the kind of nurturing father Tom aspired to be, he gave Tom far fewer disapproving looks, and occasionally voiced appreciation for Tom's keeping him informed of absences better and staying on top of key projects. The two enjoyed attending the grandchildren's games together regularly, and managed to get together without their families, for golf or a beer, about once a month. Importantly, Robert had hinted that retirement was nearer at hand than he'd thought, and that he fully supported Tom's succeeding him when the time came. Knowing that his father felt that way, Tom said, "meant the world to me."

4

Battle of the Super-Women

From suffrage to bra-burnings to military service, no one would dispute the magnitude of change women's roles have gone through in the last decades. It's hard to believe that the controversial Virginia Slims slogan, "You've Come a Long Way, Baby," debuted in 1968, over four decades ago. For family businesses, those changes have meant increasing involvement for women—as company founders, managers, employees, and supporters—often with dominant roles in both business and family. Though the term is overused, we can think of these females as "super-women," as they were the first to rise beyond stereotypical roles to take on major challenges in multiple settings, excelling in each. The presence of super-women has been a great thing for businesses in general, as they've benefited from female family members' talents. At the same time, the rapid evolution of women's roles has led to increased tension in family businesses—especially among the women, as each generation holds different expectations of themselves and other women in the family regarding motherhood, management, and other areas. This chapter will help all generations of super-women and those around them manage the issues created by their perspectives, expectations, and frustrations.

The Queen of Mean and Her Daughters-in-Law

It was a daydream Agnes Park indulged in often lately: taking her children to the zoo, hosting birthday parties for them, and bringing them to the office, where they made airplanes out of copy paper and flew them around the cubicles laughing. It wasn't that Agnes hadn't done those things; she had. But that was many years ago, in the decade after she'd arrived in Florida from Korea, newly married and excited about the life she and her husband would build together.

Raised by very traditional parents, Agnes hadn't expected that her new life would include helping to start a business. Though she excelled as a math major in college, all she had envisioned was raising children, keeping house, and enjoying time with other Korean families. But that changed the day her husband Charles, an engineering Ph.D. student, came home with what he called a "crazy idea": starting an office supply company. Charles had noticed the poor quality of office supplies in his academic department, and believed they could find and sell better ones. Though neither had any business background, the couple jumped in, learning as they went.

They became more successful than they'd thought possible. Within two years, Park Office Supplies was the premier supplier of office materials—paper, folders, writing instruments, and so forth—to several major universities and companies in Florida. As they expanded quickly, Charles left engineering to focus on the business full-time. A natural with people (he was the son of a very successful machinery salesman), he handled all marketing and business development efforts, along with maintaining relationships with major suppliers. Agnes, meanwhile, put her quantitative skills to work, overseeing finance, accounting, and operations and taking university extension courses at night to enhance her knowledge.

As the business expanded, so did the family. Agnes and Charles had three children: sons David and Joseph, with daughter Lorena between them. Agnes was determined to nurture her family and the business, taking a very active role in the children's development and schooling—including trips to the zoo and birthday parties—while maintaining long, late hours to make up for it in her work responsibilities. "I was always exhausted," she said, "but it was worth it."

Now, 65-year-old Agnes's daydream was disrupted by the phone's ring. She smiled when she saw it was David, her older son, then cringed when the call began as it often did, "Hi Mom, I was just looking over some numbers and...." David, 39, had joined the business soon after college. Like his mother, he was strong in math, and enjoyed working on finance and accounting projects. In the beginning, mother and son had spent long hours together, poring over spreadsheets and refining growth projections. Agnes remembered those times fondly, partly because they seemed too short: in his mid-twenties, David was accepted for graduate study at the University of Chicago, returning home with an MBA and a fiancée, Heidi, a classmate one year younger.

Early in David's married life, Agnes and her daughter-in-law, Heidi, worked hard to accept each other. Agnes found that she'd internalized more of her parents' traditional values than she realized, and sometimes wondered why David had chosen a spouse who wasn't Korean. Heidi, a management consultant with a busy travel schedule, was enthusiastic about learning Korean customs and cuisine, even experimenting with making spicy kimchi pickle. The situation declined when David and Heidi had their first child, and Heidi quit her job to stay home with the baby. Agnes's visits to her son's house were a mix of cooing at her grandson and making increasingly critical comments to Heidi: "When David was a baby I managed to keep the house clean *and* build a business."

As the tension between the women intensified, including some periods when the pair refused to speak, David intervened, asking his mother to take it easy on his wife. In such conversations, Agnes expressed surprise: she hadn't intended the remarks as insults. But she knew that wasn't the whole truth. Part of her animosity toward Heidi was that she was convinced her daughter-in-law had "changed" her son. No longer the little boy who held his mother's hand at the zoo or the young man who showed her a new macro to use in Excel, David, now vice president of finance for the business, seemed distant. Worse, when David came up with a new finance or operations idea, as he often did these days, Agnes felt it wasn't his idea, but Heidi's. After all, David's wife also held an MBA from one of the world's top finance programs, and had been very successful as a management consultant—she'd been firmly on the partner track when she left. Now that Heidi's children (she and David had another boy two years after the first) were in school full-time, she seemed restless and willing to return to work. But she was no longer interested in the long hours and heavy travel requirements of management consulting, and talked about taking a more flexible position. Despite having been a successful business-woman herself, Agnes was puzzled by Heidi's restlessness: "Why isn't she happy just staying home with her children?"

The situation made Agnes grateful that she and Charles had decided, soon after their children joined Park Office Supplies, that only blood relatives could hold positions with the business. The couple had heard too many stories of dam-aging divorces in the United States to trust allowing in-laws into the company they had sacrificed so much for. But in the years since, Charles had often spoken of reversing this decision, not so much for Heidi, but for Cathy, their younger son Joseph's wife. By that time, Joseph, 37, was Marketing Director for the company, working alongside his father. He'd met Cathy, his wife and a fellow Korean American, when they both worked for their college newspaper. The couple now had one daughter. Cathy had worked as an advertis-ing account executive before her child was born, and, like her father-in-law, showed great skill with client service. She and Charles often discussed challenges that the family busi-ness faced, especially as it worked with more Asian suppliers and a broader range of customers. Cathy often came up with thoughtful solutions. "So smart, that one," Charles would say, hinting to Agnes that loosening the blood-relatives-only restriction might not be a bad idea.

But Agnes held firm to the policy. She'd been so pleased when Joseph announced his engagement to Cathy, and sought to commiserate about Heidi with her younger daughter-in-law: "At least you understand our customs."

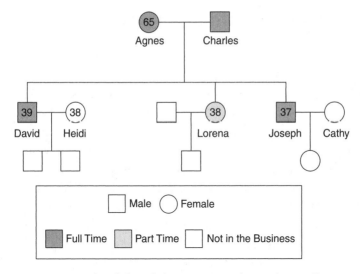

Figure 4.1   Battle of the Alpha Women: The Park Family

But she'd been dismayed to find Cathy unwilling to disparage Heidi. Adding insult to injury, Heidi was the one who had expressed more interest in Korea, even encouraging her sons to take Korean lessons and serving them traditional dishes, while Cathy showed little interest in her own heritage and fed her daughter a steady diet of hot dogs and macaroni and cheese.

Despite these differences, Heidi and Cathy had formed a close bond, partly revolving around their observations of Agnes, whom they'd dubbed the "Queen of Mean" for her perceived rigidness. Frustrated at first by the family's policy of not including in-laws in the business, the two women now felt "relieved" that they wouldn't have to work alongside Agnes. As Agnes had suspected, Heidi was indeed transmitting ideas for the business through David, but she and David had agreed not to tell his parents this, to avoid making waves. Heidi and Cathy had also learned not to push David and Joseph to serve as go-betweens in their relationships with Agnes; the men were sympathetic to their wives' situation, but wary of angering their mother. In fact, all three of the Park men tended to stay out of the family's challenging dynamics, doing their work quietly and hoping the tension would subside.

It didn't. Family get-togethers were increasingly uncomfortable, with too many conversational minefields—from business issues to housekeeping to parenting. As David said, when the extended family met, "everyone's attention was on the wrong things." The only member who'd been spared was Lorena, the middle child and only daughter. Lorena, who was married and had a son, worked part-time as an accountant for the business and helped lead its increasing philanthropy efforts (helping low-income Korean immigrant families). Lorena maintained friendly relationships with her sisters-in-law, and was particularly skilled at humoring Agnes without reinforcing her mother's feelings. "Mom," Lorena would say whenever Agnes raised a complaint about Heidi or Cathy, "I think you're expecting too much."

Agnes disagreed. She felt frustrated that no one, including Charles, understood her dissatisfaction about how distant her sons had become. So it was no surprise that she found herself daydreaming more frequently, recalling the days of zoo trips and birthday parties, when motherhood and building a business had seemed so easy.

Battle of the Super-Women: The Symptom

Families in business today enjoy many more opportunities than in the past, from using social media-based strategies to leveraging outsourcing to having more members join the business, including female relatives. But that also means a bigger battlefield, with a greater number of triggers and contentious relationships, as the Park family discovered firsthand. Disputes and dissatisfaction can arise over business issues (e.g., ownership), family issues (e.g., parenting), and issues at the intersection of these (e.g., which family members can join the business).

While the larger battlefield is related to many of the symptoms previously discussed, the symptom of focus here is what I call Battle of the Super-Women, as it relates directly to strained relationships among female family members. Agnes Park and her daughters-in-law had the potential to enjoy strong bonds as family and potentially as colleagues in Park Office Supplies. And while personality traits may have played a role in their conflicts, other, more sociological factors contributed significantly as well. Most of these were related to the fast-changing role of women in the last decades. It's a situation where progress in one area has meant new challenges in others.

Women Then and Now

The lines used to be clearer: men worked outside of the house and women worked within it. In the United States, that pattern was maintained for the most part until the middle of the twentieth century, when women began taking on jobs that had typically been dominated by men, from manufacturing to office administration, partly due to the labor shortage caused by the war. This shift to women working outside the home was accelerated and intensified by the feminist movement of the 1960s and 1970s.

By late 2009, women made up an estimated 48 percent of the U.S. workforce (up from about 30 percent in the late 1960s), and nearly two-thirds of all families had a woman as primary breadwinner or co-breadwinner (up from less than 30 percent in the late 1960s).[1] The latter figure was rising as the recession that began in late 2007 continued; more and more women were supporting or helping to support their families financially. The trend is seen as a permanent shift, rather than a short-term reaction to economic factors, in part because the jobs that women are more likely to hold are expected to rise more than those positions typically held by men.[2]

Nowhere is the trend toward women working outside the home more obvious than in the business world. The number of women-owned businesses in the United States has grown steadily, to an estimated 10.1 million in 2010, with many of these in more traditionally male-dominated fields like manufacturing and construction.[3]

Fast Fact

Women-owned firms generate an estimated $1.9 trillion in annual revenues in the United States.

Source: Leslie Kwoh, "Female Firms Venture into Male-Dominated Industries and Thrive," *The Star Ledger,* April 11, 2010 (http://www.nj.com/business/index.ssf/2010/04/female_entrepreneurs_venture_i.html) (accessed April 11, 2010).

Statistics also show, however, that female entrepreneurs and other working women face a more challenging juggling act than their male counterparts; women spend three more hours a week on childcare than men.[4] That challenge hasn't daunted women from aspiring to business roles in general; for example, 100,000 women, a record number, took the GMAT, the business-school entrance exam, in 2009, 40 percent of all test-takers.[5]

The wide-ranging implications of the trends discussed here are reflected in the title of a report commissioned by the Center for American Progress: "A Woman's Nation Changes Everything."[6] The "changes" aren't just about statistics, but roles, as illustrated by the Park family example. Leaders of the feminist movement of the 1960s and 1970s were Boomer-generation women who fought for respect and equality. Their efforts—which may well have had an effect on Agnes Park, who immigrated to the United States during that period—helped open the door to the working world for many women. But something interesting happened with this "transition" cohort of women; they seemed able to straddle the line between home and workplace better than any generation before or since. As much as they fought for liberation and equal rights, there was also an inherent comfort with a more traditional homemaker role focused on being a wife and mother. The latter role was rooted in a long history.

So it's not surprising that Agnes Park was able to "switch" easily from her role as business-builder to that of spouse and mom. Not only was she operating at a point in history when women were transitioning from at-home to working roles, but she was also from Korea, a country that emphasized traditional gender roles more so than the United States did at the time. For her daughters-in-law, it was a bit more complicated. In the chapter called Meet the MEOWs, we'll talk about all the challenges Generation X women face balancing the many roles they take on. For now, it's important to understand that Heidi and Cathy weren't comfortable being kept out of the business, and certainly resented Agnes's thinly veiled criticisms of their homemaking skills. They were also well-equipped to contribute to the business, based on their skills and experience, but were losing interest in contributing because of Agnes's opposition and attitude.

Now let's consider the presence of Battle of the Super-Women as a potential symptom in your family business.

Diagnosing Battle of the Super-Women

The list below can help you think about whether your family business shows characteristics related to Battle of the Super-Women.

IF YOU AGREE MORE THAN DISAGREE WITH THESE STATEMENTS, BATTLE OF THE SUPER-WOMEN MAY BE A SYMPTOM WORTH TREATING IN YOUR FAMILY BUSINESS.

- Our family gatherings are tense, especially due to conflicts among the women in the family.
- Younger-generation women in our family tend to feel judged about their ability to balance career and home life.
- Younger-generation women in our family don't feel that their career experience and education is respected/valued by the older generation.

- Older-generation women in our family believe that the younger-generation women are over-involved in business issues, often speaking for their spouses.
- The nuclear family in our family business rarely spends time together without the spouses (i.e., daughters-in-law).
- The level of tension among our extended family rose considerably when new female relatives (i.e., daughters-in-law) entered the picture.
- The men in our family tend to avoid conflict among the women and/or take on peacekeeping roles.

Battle of the Super-Women: The Treatment

Families must first understand the generation-based patterns they've fallen into and why. Then practical steps are developed to alter these patterns.

Understanding the Stack-Up Patterns

After considering a series of questions about their situation (see Chapter 1), families can begin to understand their specific issues within context, linking their challenges to underlying sources. The Parks needed to understand the challenges associated with the roles and expectations of the women in the family: Agnes and her daughters-in-law. Getting them to talk about their roles and wishes, and helping them place these challenges into a bigger-picture context—specifically, that the women were from different generations, which had sometimes led to clashing attitudes and expectations. All three women shared an interest in having healthy professional and at-home lives, but the messages they'd internalized from growing up when they did prevented them from seeing this as something they had in common.

Specifically, Agnes approached the situation—and her daughters-in-law—with the idea that a woman should be very comfortable shifting from a professional role to that of spouse and homemaker. Moreover, she felt that her daughters-in-law's advice about business matters—especially Heidi's—was excessive, and crossed a boundary that she preferred to keep clear. Heidi and Cathy, on the other hand, wanted more fluidity in their lives; they wanted more of a balance between professional and personal. That meant not having to dust every surface of their homes on a daily basis, as Agnes seemed to expect, and being able to contribute to the family business on a casual basis, if not a more formal one. As Gen Xers, Heidi and Cathy also wanted more immediate changes (e.g., to the family employment policy), as opposed to the older Parks, who were accustomed to more gradual change.

The Park men weren't helping matters by staying silent and trying to avoid the clashes among their wives. By taking this attitude, they were effectively condoning the conflicts—or at least signaling that it wasn't worth their time to sort through them. This element of the dynamic in this example highlights that *everyone* has a role in a family business conflict, whether they want it or not.

The process should not be about forcing individuals to change into something they aren't, but to help them understand how to work better together. Equipped with a deeper understanding of the factors contributing to the situation, we moved into changing the stack-up patterns to address the symptom of Battle of the Super-Women.

Changing the Stack-Up Patterns

The Parks could take several steps to improving their stack-up patterns.

Break unhealthy alliances. The challenges the Parks faced had led to a number of relationships that helped relieve short-term stress but exacerbated longer-term issues. Among these were connections between the daughters-in-law, attempted links between Agnes and two of the other women in the family, David and Heidi's collusion, and the shared silence of the men.

It was understandable that Heidi and Cathy would bond over their shared frustration with their mother-in-law; to some degree, it's healthy for any family member to seek support and empathy from another. But the mean-spirited element of the daughters-in-law's alliance was only distancing the two younger women from their mother-in-law. Heidi and Cathy had to do their best to take the "complaining" element out of their bond and to replace it with more proactive ideas about what they could do to feel content about the situation (e.g., growing in their outside career paths). It has to be noted that while it may have seemed hard to imagine, improvements in the family situation might allow them to eventually address these issues with Agnes herself.

The family also had positive examples of avoiding unhealthy alliances. The best one was Lorena's unwillingness to join her mother in disparaging her sisters-in-law. Lorena explained to the others why she had chosen to stay out of the harmful relationship (importantly, she had done this without just staying silent), and reinforced her reasons. Recall from the previous chapter the family-system phenomenon of "triangulation"—when two members with a difficult relationship go through a third; here, Agnes's attempts to pit other women in the family against one another to serve her needs exemplifies a process known as "splitting," or forcing two other family members into extreme roles to satisfy your own need. In this case, Agnes tried to cast Lorena as the "all good" daughter, and the wives of her sons as "all bad." The split would have helped her rationalize her petty behavior. A secondary example of positive avoidance of an unhealthy alliance (or instance of splitting) in the Park family was Cathy's failure to ally with Agnes (against Heidi) around cultural issues, though this was partly a result of Cathy's limited observation of Korean customs.

The effects of an alliance between David and Heidi was more subtle, but still had a negative impact. Specifically, by communicating Heidi's ideas for the business through David, the couple had raised Agnes's suspicion and put her in a difficult position: taking "David's" suggestions seriously when she doubted they were his in the first place. I suggested that David and Heidi adopt a policy of being upfront about where the ideas were coming from and consider having Heidi suggest them more directly, if the family situation allowed for this in the future.

Finally, the code of silence between the men, an unspoken alliance (because if one of them had spoken up about the issues, the others would likely have followed), wasn't helping, as pointed out earlier. Unfortunately, this is a typical behavior on the part of men across cultures: staying out of emotional conflicts, especially those among women. By taking themselves out of the picture, they were avoiding active roles as problem-solvers. In reality, they were central to the layers of conflict because of their dual roles: as Agnes's sons and their wives' husbands. As a result, they were in the best position to mitigate the clashes, because the women in the family valued their relationships with the Park men. The men in the family had to be honest about what they had observed in the family, and the effects this had on them, as well as pledging to take a more active role in resolving the family's issues.

Respect your roots—and let them go/grow. As Agnes had the most obvious role in driving family conflict, it would have been easy to trace all the clashes back to her. But that would have been misguided. In reality, she had a legitimate point of view: her sons had become more distant, and no one in the family understood how hard it had been for Agnes to accept how the family had changed. As Agnes said, "When a daughter marries, she brings a son to the family; when a son marries, he brings potential trouble."

Addressing this part of the family situation involved both psychological and practical elements. On the psychological front, Agnes had to accept that families evolve, and hers was no exception. New relationships mean new issues to deal with and adjustments to make. It was simplistic to believe that the entry of new women into the family was the sole reason for the challenges the Parks faced. Agnes's own attitude, expectations, and behaviors had contributed to her dissatisfaction and distanced her sons from her—a cycle she wasn't aware of. Pointing out (gently) to Agnes that in many ways she was forcing her boys to choose between their mother and the mother of their children helped her understand how that put them in a very challenging position. At the same time, I asked other members of the family to try to see the situation from Agnes's point of view, and to understand how hard it had been for her, and how they had contributed to her challenges. They had to understand the importance of their roots; a tree can't grow new branches easily if its roots are damaged.

Find the right roles. So much of the conflict within the Park family stemmed from roles individual members had—or hadn't—taken. The most obvious source of tension was the daughters-in-law's involvement in the business, whether overt or covert. Agnes was wary of either. Both Heidi and Cathy were well-equipped to make valuable contributions to the business, but their interest in doing so had waned because of the family's dynamics. What could they do?

Revisiting and/or hastily revising the blood-relatives-only employment policy wasn't the right thing to do—at least not immediately. But the family had to have the tough conversation they needed to have about the policy: why they had instituted it in the first place; how it wasn't meant as a personal insult to their daughters-in-law; and why it made sense to respect it. Heidi and Cathy were used to faster changes, given their generational context, but they had to accept a slower process of evolution in this area.

At the same time, the Parks had to think about a family business as a potluck party, where everyone brings something. Heidi had great finance and strategy skills; Cathy was highly capable with client management. It made sense to use these skills in some way for the family business—though perhaps not in management roles in the immediate future. The family was also encouraged to think about an option they may not have considered before: having the daughters-in-law involved in the growing philanthropy arm of the business, as long as this didn't violate the family employment policy. Everyone expressed enthusiasm for this idea, and they agreed to explore it more fully. Regular family meetings would be the ideal forum for such discussions.

Maintaining Changes

Six months after the treatment plan, the Parks were doing much better on several fronts. There was little evidence of the unhealthy alliances in place previously: Heidi and Cathy had committed to not complaining about Agnes; David and Heidi had agreed that they would stop communicating Heidi's ideas for the business as David's; Charles, David, and Joseph had made progress toward being more vocal in general (though their wives were generating less conflict than previously). The nuclear family had also made good on their agreement to spend more time together. The five "original" Parks enjoyed lunch together (on a weekday) once a month, and Agnes and each of her sons had lunch or went for a walk about as often. They noted that these occasions included some discussion of the business and some time spent reconnecting more generally.

With regard to finding the right roles for everyone, the family had less to report. While initially enthusiastic about the idea of helping with philanthropic efforts, Heidi and Cathy hadn't done much in this regard, partly because they continued to be busy with other activities (e.g., at the children's schools). Recall that Lorena only worked part-time on philanthropy, so there was no clear "point person" to help the daughters-in-law become more involved. At the same time, I sensed some hesitation on everyone's part to take this step, and encouraged them to explore potential reasons for that more fully, while recognizing that it was best to let any changes unfold slowly, when people felt more ready for it.

Overall, the Parks had made great progress in a short time frame, and that boded well for future improvement.

5

Meet the MEOWs—Mommy Executive Officer Women

They seem to have it all: career, family, friends, and the time and space to enjoy all of these. So why are so many Gen X women today dissatisfied? Some of the reasons parallel those of their male counterparts, including the idea that having too many choices isn't always a good thing. Other reasons, rooted in biology and historical gender roles, are more specific to women. The complication, of course, is that Gen X females facing today's challenges often have to deal with their parents who, as illustrated in the Battle of the Super-Women chapter, may hold different expectations about what women can—and can't—do. This chapter will help Gen X women and those around them gain perspective on the challenges they face and embrace personal and professional lives that are both full and satisfying.

The Perfect Girl's Imperfect Life

She was always perfect. The trophies—for sports, grades, and debates—lining the shelves of Nancy Wilkes's room were a testament to it. Nancy's record of over-achievement began in grade school and continued well beyond, including a scholarship to an Ivy League university, where she was a star in the classroom and on the soccer field. Her performance helped her secure an internship with a top New York investment bank and an invitation to return as an analyst. Post-college, Nancy distinguished herself even among her highly accomplished peers at the bank, which helped her gain admission to Harvard Business School, including sponsorship from the bank. After thriving at HBS, she returned to the bank as an associate, and was well on track to an early promotion.

One phone call changed everything. "Nancy," her father said, "we could use your help at Home Star." Home Star was the mortgage brokerage Paul Wilkes had founded when Nancy was in middle school. Starting as a regional player in the Pacific Northwest, Home Star had grown to offer home loans and home equity lines of credit to customers nationwide as the U.S. real estate market skyrocketed for most of the 2000s. By the time Nancy finished business school, her father's company employed over 50 people—including her mother and younger brother—and was growing over 30 percent annually.

The decline began seemingly overnight, in late 2007. Home prices plunged, credit markets froze, and layoffs soared. Each month, more mortgage companies vanished, including several of Home Star's competitors. Paul Wilkes's company stayed afloat, due largely to its focus on serving high-net-worth customers and a strong referral network, but he couldn't avoid layoffs, including several members of the finance department, whose salaries had grown disproportionately. At the same time, Paul saw a great opportunity to acquire some of Home Star's struggling peer companies.

When Paul called Nancy she asked, "What do you need me to do?" His reply: "Everything." He wasn't kidding. Given her track record, Paul saw his older child as capable of serving Home Star in several areas: straightening out the company's financials and putting key reporting systems in place; serving as the primary contact for several of Home Star's largest bank partners; helping Paul expand the company's strategy to include lucrative commercial real estate customers; negotiating the purchase of and integrating several acquisition targets; building on Home Star's fledgling community service efforts (e.g., partnering with local groups that helped low-income groups find housing). "I trust you to be the brains and face of this company," Paul told his daughter.

Nancy's colleagues at the bank were shocked when she announced her resignation; she was leaving a prestigious job and potential millions in near-term compensation to join a small business in a struggling industry. "I'm doing it for family," she said. "And I can always come back." In reality, she had other motivations for the career change. One of the biggest was fatigue: investment bankers are notorious for the hours they put in, and Nancy worked harder than most of her peers, sometimes going weeks on only two or three hours of sleep nightly. She saw working for the family business as an opportunity for a much better work-life balance, including more time with her husband, Rick, an attorney who worked in public defense. Nancy, by then in her early thirties, was on the verge of having her own family; she and Rick had been trying for their first child for several months. Nancy saw how little time her colleagues spent with their children, and wanted to avoid that for herself. She also liked the idea of living closer to home, especially so that her future children could get to know their grandparents and uncle better. Nancy's mother, Alice, who worked part-time for Home Star in accounting, and her brother, Randy, a sales manager for the company, told her how excited they were to have her come back. Smiling, Nancy said goodbye to New York.

At first it seemed the best decision of her life. Within six months, Nancy had whipped Home Star's finances into shape, made strong connections with established and prospective bank partners, helped acquire two competitors, and formulated a strong vision for growth with her father. In a desert of dying mortgage brokers, Home Star was a green oasis of profits, and Paul gave Nancy much of the credit for this, including at all-company meetings. Nancy had also made progress with the company's community service efforts, appearing on the front page of a local newspaper in

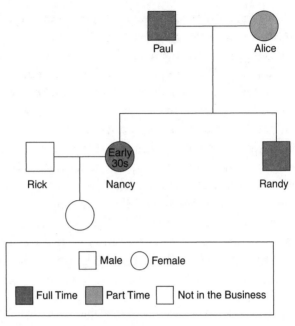

Figure 5.1 Meet the MEOWs—Mommy Executive Officer Women: The Wilkes Family

a picture of the groundbreaking for a new public housing development Home Star had invested in. On top of her professional success, Nancy was pregnant with her first child.

The good times didn't last. A year later, the economic downturn had worsened, and the mortgage industry remained one of its largest casualties. Home Star's success after Nancy's arrival had been built largely on the new business it gained from its acquisitions; these revenue sources tapered off quickly. Yet the company managed to stay solvent by laying off one-third of its workforce and cutting its commission rates deeply. Several of the growth initiatives Nancy had helped craft ground to a halt—for example, as the commercial real estate market stagnated, Paul and Nancy agreed that it was best to hold off entering that area. But Paul encouraged Nancy to think broadly in generating solutions. "Take all the space you need," he said, assuring his daughter that he trusted her judgment.

Nancy's reaction was to push harder—on every dimension. Soon she was putting in about as many hours as she had in banking, calling after-hour strategy meetings, poring over spreadsheets well past midnight, and urging Home Star's remaining staff to "be creative." Her colleagues began to push back, and one finance person even left the company, noting how the company's environment had become "much more rigid and full of unrealistic expectations." Nancy's brother Randy, known for his people skills and laid-back style as a manager, confronted her directly: "You're approaching this like a robot; it's not like there's a 'formula' that will solve everything." She retorted that he "just wasn't willing to put in the time to do it right." Alice, her mother, focused on a different issue, mentioning "how nice" it would be to have another grandchild and hinting that Nancy wasn't getting any younger. Nancy's response was to remind Alice how hard Alice had fought for "equal rights"—she'd told Nancy about all the marches she'd joined in the 1970s, and how much pride she took in being a homemaker *and* a professional.

But Nancy's biggest critic was herself. In her view, she was failing both at work and at home. For all of her effort, Home Star continued to struggle, and her colleagues were resistant to working anywhere near as hard as she did. Though no one would have guessed, Nancy lacked confidence in herself and her ideas, which was part of her motivation to work even harder. On top of that, the work-life balance she was hoping to maintain by joining the family business had disappeared. At first, she had been able to keep to a very specific schedule of professional and personal activities (e.g., a "date night" every Friday and one weeknight to catch up with old friends), but soon began to sacrifice family time for late hours at the office. Rick spent more and more time alone with their daughter (as he reminded Nancy frequently), date nights and social events became a thing of the past and, though the couple had talked often about having another child, it was hard for Nancy to imagine taking on any other responsibilities. In fact, she now thought that it was actually easier to exist at one extreme or the other—full-time mother or hard-working banker—than living the "balanced" life she supposedly had. But the reality was that overachiever Nancy wouldn't have been happy staying at home and rejoining her investment bank would be virtually impossible, given the layoffs in that industry. The rare times she stopped by the home she grew up in, Nancy looked wistfully at the trophies in her old room, remembering how easy it had seemed to have "everything" back in those days.

Meet the MEOWs: The Symptom

If Gen X women are supposed to have it "all," why do so many feel that they have so little? Freedom for women—with regard to family and career, especially in highly developed countries like the United States—may be unprecedented, but many of today's 30- and 40-something females are too busy trying to play too many roles to see themselves as "free." Rather, they're trapped by their own expectations of "having it all," society's view of what women's roles should be today, and, often, previous generations' perceptions and biases, especially those of their mothers.

In the last chapter I mentioned the old Virginia Slims slogan "You've Come a Long Way, Baby" in the context of how much women's roles have changed in recent decades. The challenges Gen X women face today warrant adding a second part to that: "You've Come a Long Way, Baby—Are You Sure You Want to Be Here?" What Gen X women are up against is captured nicely by what I named this chapter's symptom of focus: Meet the MEOWs—Mommy Executive Officer Women. Women in their thirties and forties today are supposed to embody all three parts of that phrase, not necessarily in the order mentioned: they're supposed to fulfill their roles as moms (not just having children but taking active part in their lives), career-oriented people (more and more in high-level leadership roles, especially in smaller business like those run by families), and women (liberated free spirits who can be whatever they want to be). But as Nancy Wilkes found out, life as a MEOW was more complicated than she expected, to the point that she concluded that living just one part of MEOW—either as a mommy (full-time mother) or an executive officer (ascending within investment banking)—might have been preferable to having it all. Let's take a closer look at why women like Nancy face the challenges they do.

Three Steps Forward, Two Steps Back

There's no question that women are succeeding on more fronts than ever. Today's women represent an unprecedented percentage of the workforce and the majority of families now include a woman as primary or co-breadwinner. The educational and economic portrait of the typical family, then, has changed a lot in the last decades. In 1970, men made up nearly two-thirds of college graduates in a U.S. sample; in 2007, this proportion had dropped to just under 47 percent—for the first time, women made up the majority of college graduates.[1] With regard to economics, in 1975 45 percent of households were "traditional," where the man was the only one employed outside the home; by 2008, that number had dropped by more than half, to 21 percent.[2] And that figure was expected to continue declining as the global recession deepened, disproportionately affecting jobs held by men.[3]

Fast Fact

In 1970, 4 percent of men had wives who made more money than they did. In 2007, 22 percent did.

Source: Nicole Santa Cruz, "Women Out-earning, Out-learning Men in More Couples," *Los Angeles Times*, January 20, 2010 (http://articles.latimes.com/2010/jan/20/nation/la-na-marriage20–2010jan20) (accessed April 19, 2010).

The success of women in the workplace has even prompted some researchers to argue that marriage today represents "a way for men to achieve economic security."[4]

Unfortunately, while expectations of women in the working world—by men, society in general, and women themselves—have risen, we haven't seen a corresponding decline in expectations of women at home; one study found that in couples where women earned more than their husbands, the husbands didn't contribute more at home than in marriages where the men earned more.[5] This converges with evidence I presented in the Battle of the Super-Women chapter: that working women still spend more weekly hours on childcare than working men.

So one way to think about the situation for women today is that they face all the expectations they did in traditional roles as nurturing homemakers *and* many of the expectations that used to be the more exclusive domain of men—the idea that they should be seeking higher education and higher incomes. It's not surprising that this "freedom" doesn't taste as sweet as women fighting for equality in years past might have hoped. In fact, as discussed in the Battle of the Super-Women chapter, a complicating factor for Gen X women is that their mothers don't understand their struggles because the older generation—mostly Boomers—had the "luxury" of being able to play both traditional male and female roles without being *expected* to play both. And women today are struggling to meet these social expectations with lower overall levels of confidence than men—most likely forged by society in the first place—in domains from investing to politics to education, even though performance levels between genders are typically indistinguishable.[6]

What are the real-life implications of all this stress for women today? One is the set of scary and surprising statistics about women's health; for example, since 1984, more women than men have died annually from heart disease, and this gap is widening.[7] Less surprisingly, women are waiting longer to have children as they juggle career ambition with more traditional family roles; the average age for a women at the birth of her first child has risen three years since 1970.[8] Perhaps most remarkably, life expectancy is dropping for a significant percentage of women: for up to 19 percent of women in the U.S., compared to only 4 percent of men.[9] The discrepancy is blamed largely on high rates of smoking, obesity, and other conditions, many of which can be stress-related.[10]

To place the discussion in more of a generational context, the trends above have only exacerbated Gen X's tendency toward skepticism and mistrust of traditional structures—both at work and at home. After all, this is a cohort of people that bore witness to a tripling of the divorce rate and a rampant rise in technology that made life both more convenient and more complicated.[11] Nancy Wilkes typifies Gen X women in the challenges she faces, including her struggle to succeed as a professional, wife, mother, and daughter. In the end, this MEOW felt she was failing on every count: as mommy, executive, and woman.

Now let's consider Meet the MEOWs as a potential symptom in your family business.

Diagnosing Meet the MEOWs

The list below can help you think about whether your family business shows characteristics related to Meet the MEOWs.

IF YOU AGREE MORE THAN DISAGREE WITH THESE STATEMENTS, MEET THE MEOWS MAY BE A SYMPTOM WORTH TREATING IN YOUR FAMILY BUSINESS.

- Women in our business feel they are not performing adequately in their roles as employees/managers, mothers, wives, and in other areas.
- There is a rigidness to the boundaries in the lives/schedules of women in our business—little flexibility in work and home life.
- Women in our business tend to feel misunderstood by other women in the business/family—that their individual challenges and contributions aren't appreciated.

- Women in our business tend to set unrealistic expectations of themselves with regard to their performance in the roles they hold.
- Couples in our business rarely spend time alone together—it's either work time or family time.
- People in our business feel disconnected from some of the female family employees because they see them as overbearing or hard to get to know.
- Women in our business lack confidence in themselves despite strong records of achievement.

Meet the MEOWs: The Treatment

Families must first understand the generation-based patterns they've fallen into and why. Then practical steps are developed to alter these patterns.

Understanding the Stack-Up Patterns

After considering a series of questions about their situation (see Chapter 1), families can begin to understand their specific issues within a context, linking their challenges to underlying sources. For the Wilkeses, highlighting the challenges associated with the roles and expectations of family members, especially Nancy and her parents, meant talking about their roles and wishes, and understanding these in a bigger-picture context. As a Gen X overachiever, Nancy was placing unrealistic expectations on herself, and these were being exacerbated by both of her parents. Her father, a nice guy who had been a longtime supporter of women's rights and champion of his daughter's capabilities, had given her too much space and fed directly into her self-expectations by urging her to do "everything." Her mother had failed to appreciate the weight of expectation Nancy—and society—were placing on her and thus minimized her daughter's struggle, along with pressuring her to take on a more traditional role (i.e., having another child) without sacrificing her contributions to the business. The family was using mixed messages—all in the name of "support"—and this made a hard situation even more challenging for Nancy.

It was important that Nancy not place even more pressure on herself by willing herself to "change" into something she wasn't. It was unlikely that Nancy would ever lose her drive to succeed at work and at home, no matter how many children she had or how much Home Star grew. At the same time, if she didn't gain some perspective and self-awareness and take some practical steps, she was minimizing her chances—and her family's—to feel fulfilled and perform optimally.

Equipped with a deeper understanding of the factors contributing to the situation, we moved into changing the stack-up patterns to address the symptom of Meet the MEOWs.

Changing the Stack-Up Patterns

Plan realistically. Though they may have seemed realistic, many of the Wilkeses' plans—at work and at home—weren't. They needed to achieve better balance in several areas. For example, Nancy was set up to fail from the start, given her and Paul's expectations of her: to do "everything." When can you check "everything" off your list or proclaim "mission accomplished" and mean it? That's right: never. Unfortunately, this setup played right into Nancy's natural drive and how she'd learned to operate in investment banking's notorious culture where "good enough" is a misnomer: good is never enough. That mentality is directly at odds with the culture of most family businesses, which strive for balance in multiple dimensions, so it's no surprise that Nancy started rubbing her colleagues the wrong way as she pushed harder and harder.

I pointed out these patterns to the family, especially Nancy and her father, and urged them to develop clearer, more realistic expectations and plans. For example, when she first arrived to work at the business, Nancy and Paul should have sat down and laid out specific, achievable goals in multiple areas: financial systems, acquisitions, bank partner relationships, community service. Even better, they could have streamlined her initial responsibilities as she got to know her way around the business and helped others become comfortable with her; she could have focused only on acquisitions in the beginning, for example.

The same idea applies to home life, as well: keep things simple and realistic. When Nancy told me about the rigid schedule she had put up on the refrigerator—with color codes for work, family, community service, and social events—it was another way of setting herself up for failure. If she missed even one scheduled event (like one of the weekly date nights), it meant she hadn't succeeded. Nancy needed to be reminded that there was nothing wrong with aiming for goals, and that it was important to set them. But her way of doing it—with highly unrealistic targets—was just adding stress to an already stressful situation. Since she was never going to be the kind of person to stop mapping out goals, she needed to write down what she thought was realistic, and then to set the actual goal of *one-fourth* of what she thought possible: instead of four date nights a month, she should aim for one. This was very uncomfortable for Nancy, who was used to setting stretch targets and surpassing them, but she agreed to try. Nancy's husband Rick also needed to get more involved in the goal-setting; a naturally less structure-seeking person, he had learned to leave it all up to Nancy, which was clearly no longer working. In both professional and personal domains, plans are not set in stone, but meant to be refined and revised, especially when it becomes clear they might be unrealistic. This was again a foreign concept to Nancy, but she agreed to try.

Unlock compartments. Many of the Gen X women have a skill they're often unaware of: compartmentalizing. They've locked every aspect of their work, home, and psychological lives into separate boxes, and they try desperately to keep them this way. It's like they're conductors in charge of trains with boxcars carrying materials that will explode if they come into contact with one another. In reality, compartmentalizing is a way of avoiding the trade-offs inherent in life. When we're younger, we can do "everything" that fulfills us—school, part-time work, athletics, time with friends—without necessarily compartmentalizing, largely because we don't have the responsibilities around work and family that take up the majority of our adult lives. So Nancy's ability to excel in every area was doomed to disappear when she had a baby. And it did.

Nancy needed to unlock the compartments she'd created in several dimensions. The first was time: she simply wasn't going to be able to do everything at once anymore. That meant she had to distinguish between things that could wait and those that couldn't. Leading Home Star's community service efforts, along with initiatives in multiple key business areas, was something that could possibly wait for later in life, especially if she decided to spend more time with her children. Having more children was something that possibly couldn't wait, given that Nancy was already in her mid-thirties.

The second dimension to decompartmentalize was space. Without realizing it, Nancy had completely separated her home and work lives, even though she worked in a family business, where such boundaries are typically much more flexible. When she lamented not being able to see her daughter much, I asked if she'd ever brought her to work. Nancy looked at me as if she still worked in the investment bank, where children were only abstract concepts. Similarly, she had defined events like date night as something that had to take place outside the house. In reality, the few nights she made it home at a reasonable hour, she was often exhausted and couldn't imagine going out. So I urged her and Rick to try an at-home date night, even if it just meant renting a movie and ordering food in.

The final dimension of compartmentalization we discussed was people. Nancy had categorized her colleagues, including younger brother Randy, as "productive" or "unproductive," based largely on whether they were willing to burn the midnight oil, as she did. Not surprisingly, very few fell into the "productive" category. Nancy began refining her view of her coworkers, mostly by using sub-categories of their abilities to think about them: people skills, quantitative skills, teamwork, and the like. In this way, she saw how well-liked Randy was by his customers and colleagues, and began thinking about ways to leverage these qualities, rather than seeing him as lazy or inefficient. She also subjected herself to the same assessment to help her see her own areas of improvement.

Seek mentors. At the investment bank, Nancy had benefited from a senior partner who had gone out of his way to provide advice and encouragement. At the family business, she had no mentors, because her father had given her too-wide latitude and her mother had minimized her struggle. I suggested that Nancy find one or more mentors—possibly one for each important area of life. We thought about who might fit the bill, and came up with two: her aunt (Alice's sister), a successful entrepreneur who wrote music and hiked all over the world, and one of her good friends, who had left investment banking to stay home full-time with her kids. Nancy felt that her aunt could help her understand (and achieve) what made for a better work-life balance and that her friend might illuminate the rewards and challenges of making the ultimate tradeoff of work for home life.

Nancy also needed to find more common ground with her mother and to share more of her challenges with Alice, learning from her mother's perspective and experience while helping her mother to understand some of the unique pressures Gen X women faced. Nancy and her mother were excited about trying to reconnect in this way.

Maintaining Changes

Like most families I work with, the Wilkeses took their treatment plan seriously and implemented much of it. Six months later, Nancy seemed much more relaxed overall.

After our discussion, she and her father had developed a set of "achievable" goals in two areas of the business: acquisitions and financial systems. They saw these as the most urgent for the business to tackle. Nancy felt that setting a small number of goals had allowed her to approach them on a deeper level, and to understand their costs and benefits more fully. For example, she had decided against pursuing an acquisition target because that gave her more time to explore the opportunity and identify some weak financials she might have overlooked in a rush to finalize the transaction.

Similarly, Nancy had made some progress with compartmentalization. She had brought her daughter to work on several occasions, and found that having her there helped her keep the job in perspective and take some time to bond with her colleagues. Nancy had also learned a lot from seeing Randy in a more balanced way—she mentioned that she'd adopted some of his approach to people, and that he'd taken some advice from her on structuring his presentations to prospective customers more clearly. Paul reported that other Home Star employees seemed more comfortable with Nancy, in part because she had become more relaxed about her boundaries and stopped judging them based primarily on their willingness to put in long hours.

Nancy said that she'd been reluctant to contact her identified mentors much. "We just seem so different," she said. "And it's hard to find the time." I suggested that making these discussions another chore or checklist item to complete was the last thing that we wanted, but that it might still be of value to reach out to people whose perspective she admired, especially if it contrasted somewhat with her own. Nancy also mentioned that she hadn't been able to discuss expectations frankly with her mother in the six months.

At the same time, both mother and daughter were very happy about one new development: Nancy and Rick were expecting their second child. The couple had decided that having another child was their top priority, and they'd managed to spend more time together, largely because Nancy had become more relaxed about work. Now when Nancy saw her old trophies she thought of them not so much as reminders of how easy "doing everything" once was, but as symbols of how much a person could achieve with commitment, discipline, and perspective.

6

Boomer Retirement Mirage

It's something most of us dream about: shedding all responsibilities except for vacationing, playing cards, and spending time with friends and loved ones. So why has retirement become such a complicated thing? Boomers are finding out the reasons firsthand as they struggle with the economic and psychological complications of leaving the workforce, from trying to stretch savings accounts over longer periods to dealing with loneliness and identity issues. For Boomers and their business families, it can be even more challenging, given how many issues they face regarding shifting roles, responsibilities, succession, and finances. The result, naturally, is confusion and frustration for everyone, especially when retirement is more a mirage than a reality. This chapter will help you cope with Boomers' retirement-related issues, whether retirement is a mirage, a reality, or something in between.

The Mattress Prince Tries to Rest

"All I need is a desk in the corner." That's what Sam Greenberg told his son Karl two years ago, when he left Bob's Beds and More, the Southern California-based business he'd helped grow into a giant discount furniture retailer. Karl, Sam's middle child, was to become CEO of the company, the third Greenberg to hold the role.

Bob Greenberg, the Bob of Bob's Beds and More, was Sam's father and Karl's grandfather. He'd started the company as a young man in the 1950s, soon after immigrating to the United States from Israel. The business began literally out of the back of Bob's van, from which he sold cheap mattresses he'd purchased in bulk. A workaholic entrepreneur, Bob had several businesses going at once, including part ownership of a laundromat and a service that sold and delivered gas grills. But the mattresses sold best, and Bob chose to focus his energy there. Soon he had a retail store featuring mattresses, bed frames, bedroom furniture, and dinette sets. Bob was known for negotiating tough deals with manufacturers, contracts that allowed him to offer steep discounts to a growing customer base.

Of Bob's three children—Sam and a younger brother and sister—only Sam showed much interest in the business. "You're going to be a tough negotiator, son," Bob would say to Sam. "Just like your pop." He encouraged Sam to join the business and, after several years working in sales and marketing for other companies, his son did. Sam's skills helped them grow the business quickly, opening stores across Southern California and earning the father-son duo the nicknames of the Mattress King and Prince.

By his late fifties, Bob had saved more than enough to retire comfortably. Yet it was clear to Sam that his father had no intention of doing that. Ideas, advice, and vetoes still flowed freely from Bob's corner office, often to Sam's dismay. For years Sam had been trying to convince his father to expand the business to Northern California, but Bob had resisted, having become less willing to take risks as he aged.

In fact, Sam didn't have the chance to implement many of his major ideas until about 15 years later, when Bob slumped over his desk in that corner office, dead of a heart attack at 75. Sam's own children were grown by then, and he wanted them to be part of the business. Moreover, he didn't want to do what Bob had done; Sam vowed to leave the business "on a high note," rather than clinging on to the very end. Part of Sam's motivation was his many interests beyond work.

Unlike his father, who seemed to live for financial statements and negotiations, Sam enjoyed woodworking, hiking, and traveling with Liz, his wife, who was very active in book clubs and other social groups.

With this in mind, as Sam approached his mid-fifties, he announced at a family gathering that he planned to retire "before 60," and wanted one or more of the children to lead the business into the future. It seemed any of the three third-generation Greenbergs was up to the challenge: each was an achiever with a capital "A," having excelled in academics and athletics. They were also highly competitive among themselves, with Greenberg family trips often revolving around skiing ("Race you to the bottom!" was a popular phrase on these outings) and other high-intensity activities. When Sam made his announcement about retiring, oldest daughter, Ana, was climbing the corporate ladder as a pharmaceutical marketing manager, middle child Karl was moving fast

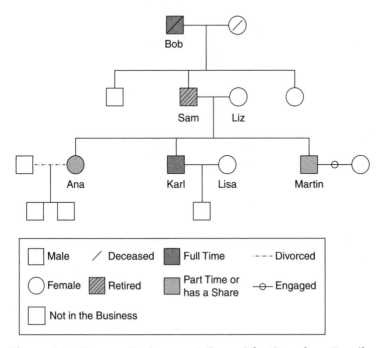

Figure 6.1   Boomer Retirement Mirage: The Greenberg Family

in his manufacturing sales career, and youngest son Martin was pursuing a Ph.D. in chemistry.

As the Greenberg siblings considered their father's proposal, each took into account elements of his or her personal life: Ana had two children and had just undergone a difficult divorce resulting in joint custody; Karl had been married to Lisa for three years, and they'd just had their first child, a son; Martin had become engaged to his fiancée in the past year. Martin quickly took himself out of the running, as he planned to pursue a career in academia. Ana and Karl discussed the possibility of working together to run the business, but ultimately decided that Karl should take over for their father, with Ana in a consulting role, to "keep things simple" for her, given her family situation. The siblings agreed to have regular family meetings to discuss any issues that came up, including finances.

Karl joined the business in the mid-2000s, and the company boomed (they'd expanded to Northern California by then) to the point that Sam was able to retire three years later with a very healthy nest egg. True to his word, he transferred his nameplate from the corner office—the same room his father Bob had occupied—to a desk in the corner. Sam and Liz bought a condo in Palm Springs and began spending more and more time there, with additional trips for hiking, Broadway plays, and international tours. Sam built all the birdhouses and other wooden objects he'd ever dreamed of. He also checked in regularly with Karl, who was implementing several digital marketing strategies that seemed promising.

The problems began about a year after Sam officially retired. The simplest issue was boredom. Sam and Liz had an increasingly difficult time finding things to do. The trips and pastimes they'd always enjoyed became "monotonous" when they did them weekly instead of monthly. "We've practically circled the world already," Liz said. And as healthy individuals nearing 60, they were hard-pressed to find friends and acquaintances within 10 years of their age among the retired set. "Whenever I call a friend he says he has to work," Sam said. The couple also found that they weren't used to dealing with each other so often; they'd always gotten along well, but were accustomed to spending most of their time apart, which had helped them appreciate each other (and avoid getting irritated by the other's habits). Sam's sense of identity was also suffering, as his work had taken up such a large part of his life, and he'd truly enjoyed most of his responsibilities, including dealing with employees, customers, and suppliers. He had begun calling Karl more often and "dropping by" to check on the business, sitting at his desk and talking to whomever happened to be around. He also made occasional visits to suppliers he'd known for decades; these interactions were ostensibly to say "hello," but Sam almost always talked business, too. Sometimes these conversations revealed that while everyone liked Karl, some thought he was still a bit inexperienced to be running the company.

Another issue was money. As the furniture industry became increasingly crowded with competitors, including big-name department stores and discount retailers like Wal-Mart and Target, the effect on the Greenbergs was multifold: Sam began advising Karl more extensively, including about the possibility of closing several stores, which seemed inevitable; the family began to worry that there weren't enough proceeds from the business to go around anymore—Karl's family relied solely on the business for income, while Ana enjoyed a nice consulting retainer and she and Martin received regular dividends from the shares they owned. Like many, Sam and Liz lost a significant part of their savings in the economic downturn at the end of the 2000s' first decade, and they were concerned about how to cover the 30 more years they might live. Sam had even begun hinting that he could "draw a salary again," or at least some consulting fees on top of the generous departure package he'd created for himself. Moreover, Sam had avoided discussing a clear plan for shifting ownership of the business to Karl and other next-generation family members—"The details can wait," he always said when Karl raised the matter. And the family reported that family meetings lacked clear agendas, and typically weren't very productive.

In general, the social and financial challenges Sam faced made him wonder if he'd retired too early. Karl, concerned about the business's future and whether he had made the right choice in taking over from his father, said little in response to Sam's hints and comments. He'd also begun to feel overwhelmed about managing Bob's Beds & More through the challenges ahead. Meanwhile, at home, Karl's wife, Lisa, reminded him of how many bills they had to pay, including their son's private school tuition, and how they'd probably never have the "luxury life" that his parents enjoyed.

So Greenberg family gatherings, once the happiest of affairs, became much more somber. Though there were few outright arguments, tensions simmered beneath family members' tight smiles. Sam was second-guessing Karl with increasing frequency, Karl was chafing against his father's intrusiveness and financial arrangement with the business, and everyone was worried that the money wouldn't last.

Boomer Retirement Mirage: The Symptom

The Greenbergs' story is becoming increasingly common: retirement, something taken for granted in years past, complicates the family business situation for everyone, on multiple levels. Often, retirement remains an abstraction rather than a reality, which is why I call this symptom Boomer Retirement Mirage—retirement seems just ahead, but never really materializes.

Note the similarities between the Greenbergs' story and that of Sterling Transportation in the chapter on Control Beyond the Grave. In both, an early-generation family business leader clings to his role for longer than is ideal for himself and the family. Sam Greenberg tried to avoid this symptom and seemed poised to: he had a healthy marriage and enough outside-of-work interests and money to make a go of retirement. It didn't work; Sam and his family found that the idea of leaving the workforce permanently was more mirage than reality.

Several economic and psychological factors combined to make this the case. Let's take a look at these.

The Death of an American Dream

Today's harsh economic realities are crushing the American Dream of putting our proverbial feet up. In early 2010, over 70 percent of U.S. workers over 60 said they were delaying retirement because they couldn't afford it; that was up from about 60 percent just two years earlier.[1] Respondents also cited the need to maintain healthcare and other benefits as a reason to keep working.

And there's no reason to expect these patterns to diminish. Two major factors explain the need to prolong work: longer lives and lower bank balances. I've already discussed in earlier chapters how much longer we're living worldwide. In fact, our longer, healthier lifespans form the foundation of the Tower of Babel that generational stack-up is—family businesses wouldn't be facing the symptoms in this book if we didn't live this long. The practical implication of longer lives is that we need to save much more money to retire comfortably—and we can no longer rely on pensions to provide these funds.

Fast Fact

In 1983, 62 percent of people in the United States were relying on pensions for retirement; in 2007, only 17 percent were.

Source: Anna Rappaport and Terry Kozlowski, "Future Patterns of Work and Retirement," World Future Society Presentation, July 2009 (http://www.wfs.org/wfs2009RetirementPDF.pdf) (accessed April 25, 2010).

Not only do fewer people even have pensions in the first place, but retirement savings of all types have been washed away by the tide of the global economic recession that began in late 2007. Even by the end of 2008, an estimated 2 trillion dollars in retirement funds had vanished.[2] In less than two years we went from a nation where the biggest challenge for many was what color to paint their new vacation home to a country where millions were newly out of work and considering moving in with friends and relatives—if they hadn't already. While Sam Greenberg's situation wasn't quite so dire, he and Liz were definitely concerned that their savings wouldn't last the decades they might need it to, especially because they were used to spending more freely than most couples their age.

But before we attribute Boomer Retirement Mirage solely to economic factors, let's not forget the psychology of leaving the workforce. In many ways, we're no longer "built to retire" as early as before—or at all—largely because we enjoy our work and it is a more important part of our identity than for previous generations. For example, the same survey that showed that many are delaying retirement because they couldn't afford it also revealed that the majority of those postponing retirement enjoyed working and weren't ready to stop.[3] And it is well-documented that having multiple roles—including parent, professional, volunteer, and so forth—is linked to better health outcomes across the lifespan.[4] So the new American Dream for our later years appears to be a mix of working, relaxing, volunteering, and socializing. Perhaps most telling—and startling—in this regard are statistics showing that men who retired early died sooner than those who waited to leave the workforce.[5] So it shouldn't be surprising that a 2007 survey showed that nearly one third of "retirees" surveyed had worked at least part-time in the previous year.[6] Many Boomers, then, not only have to work more years to make ends meet, but they enjoy what they do, and maintaining some connection to the working world is good for their health.

Sam Greenberg found this out the hard way, when he tried to make a somewhat clean break from his work life. Not only did he and Liz face challenges filling their days and dealing with each other 24/7—something they'd never done before—but he discovered an unexpected issue: the lack of social opportunities. For many of us, especially those with adult children, work life is our primary social forum, where we interact with colleagues, partners, and customers daily. When Sam left Bob's Beds, he gave up these social interactions. And he found that his friends weren't nearly as available as he was—because they were still working. Surveys show that friendships are right up there with health and finances in determining how happy retirees are.[7] Had Sam had more friends in his situation, he may not have felt as compelled to spend time at the business, where he had begun stepping on Karl's toes.

As a final note, Boomer Retirement Mirage is especially remarkable for how many people will be facing it in coming years. As noted in the first chapter, over 10,000 Boomers will become eligible for Social Security and Medicare *daily* for the next 20 years.[8] Many of these individuals, including those with family businesses, will consider retirement around the time they reach this milestone. So understanding what they and their families are up against is crucial.

Diagnosing Boomer Retirement Mirage

The list below can help you think about whether your family business shows characteristics related to Boomer Retirement Mirage.

IF YOU AGREE MORE THAN DISAGREE WITH THESE STATEMENTS, BOOMER RETIREMENT MIRAGE MAY BE A SYMPTOM WORTH TREATING IN YOUR FAMILY BUSINESS

- Earlier-generation family members still occupy offices or desks at the business though "officially" retired.
- Older-generation family members are still drawing a salary or other significant compensation from the business without clearly defined responsibilities.

- Younger-generation family members look forward to periods when earlier generation-members will be away (or dread the periods they are present).
- There is concern about the business's ability to provide sufficient funds for the older generation's retirement and the younger generation's income.
- The older generation has a clear retirement plan (e.g., where they will live and what they plan to do) that goes well beyond the next five years.
- Earlier-generation members have clear roles and/or pursuits other than those related to the business (e.g., volunteering, hobbies).
- There is little clarity on the expected role of earlier-generation members (e.g., in day-to-day operations; as board members) after they stop having official management positions.
- There is no clear process for transfer of ownership of the business between generations.
- There is no clear, agreed-upon valuation of the business (or agreed-upon process for assessing the business's value) in place.

Boomer Retirement Mirage: The Treatment

Families must first understand the generation-based patterns they've fallen into and why. Then practical steps are developed to alter these patterns.

Understanding the Stack-Up Patterns

After considering a series of questions about their situation (see Chapter 1), families can begin to understand their specific issues within a context, linking their challenges to underlying sources. For the Greenbergs, this meant highlighting the challenges associated with the roles and expectations of family members, especially as related to Sam's role in the business and money issues. Getting them to talk about their roles and wishes helped place these in bigger-picture context. Like many Boomers, Sam was stuck between work and retirement—he believed he was ready for retirement (and desperately wanted to avoid repeating his father's mistake of clinging to control), but hadn't taken into account the challenges that not working involved. Similarly, by pushing Karl to take over for him as early as possible, Sam had thrust his middle child into a role he wasn't quite ready for, given his limited experience as a manager. And the rest of the extended family was only adding to the challenges Sam and Karl faced by bringing up financial challenges regularly.

In initial meetings with the Greenbergs, it was emphasized that they were doing the right thing by grappling with these difficult problems, rather than avoiding them. While acknowledging that furniture market factors and the overall economy might improve, some of the basic challenges they faced—especially those around Sam's role in the business—would likely persist. So it was important to take several steps toward developing a healthier, more systematic way of dealing with the interconnected issues.

Equipped with a deeper understanding of the factors contributing to the situation, we moved into changing the stack-up patterns to address the symptom of Boomer Retirement Mirage.

Changing the Stack-Up Patterns

Set clear boundaries. The family had to define a clear set of roles and responsibilities for members, to avoid the confusion and frustration inevitable with overlapping roles and/ or poorly defined responsibilities. Sam's role was the most obvious one requiring better clarity. We discussed how his exiting the business didn't have to mean a complete shut-off of his involvement in it. At the same time, retirement wasn't a license to "meddle" in the company's daily operations and drop in unannounced on the business and key partners and customers. By doing this, he was preventing Karl from facing the challenges he needed to face to step fully into his role as CEO; moreover, Sam was preventing himself from facing the challenges of retirement, including dealing with his marriage and finding enough to do each day, as part of a longer-term plan.

After several difficult conversations about boundaries, we discussed what kind of role made the most sense for Sam to have. The idea that the company might need a board of directors was also raised; they had an advisory board already, but that wasn't enough. Board member was a natural role for Sam. In this way, he could stay very connected to the business without having to be involved in its daily operations. The family considered this option seriously, and in the meantime explored having Sam work on specific projects and issues, again with clear boundaries. For example, he could pitch in on thinking about finance issues—especially given the challenging economic environment—but leave operations, business development, and other areas to Karl and the rest of the management team.

Sam wasn't the only one who needed a clearer role. Ana's vague responsibilities as "consultant" were also causing stress, as no one knew exactly what she was being paid for, and it was clear that she wasn't doing much consulting with the business as had been hoped, given the full-time work and child care she had to juggle. Ana and Karl worked together to formulate a "contract" stipulating her responsibilities more clearly, including goals, success criteria, guidelines for reducing/increasing her role and compensation as needed, and escalation procedures (e.g., resolving disputes through an outside mediator). Both agreed to enforce it.

We also talked about how Martin's pressuring of the family to keep generating dividends was detrimental for everyone. In earlier times, when business was booming, it had been easy to accommodate everyone's financial needs; that was no longer the case. While the implication wasn't that Martin had to take an active management role in the business (that likely would have caused even more frustration), it seemed reasonable to expect that he would be involved in some capacity. I suggested considering responsibilities related to the business's philanthropy or community service, especially those related to education, given Martin's academic focus.

We agreed that family meetings provided the perfect forum for discussing these boundary-related issues—as long as they were part of a better-defined agenda.

Don't avoid money issues. "Do we have to talk about this?" many business families say or imply when I bring up financial issues. The short answer is yes, absolutely. Ironically, many business family members are more than willing to complain about finances, especially when business is slow, but they're reluctant to discuss money directly and reasonably with the extended family, partly because this means making tradeoffs. The Greenbergs were no different: Sam admitted that he had been purposefully vague about financial arrangements because he thought it might cause discord among his children and because he wasn't sure how much money he and Liz would need to cover their retirement years. This kind of plan (or lack thereof) can work in the short term, but almost always falls apart over time—often taking the family with it. Moreover, it was clear that no one was fully satisfied with the financial arrangement as it was.

The Greenbergs had to face some tough questions about money: What are our collective and individual financial goals? Can the business realistically address these? What kinds of tradeoffs are we willing to make collectively and individually? Helping them talk through these and set clearer budgets and goals allowed Sam and Liz had to tone down their lifestyle (e.g., fewer international trips) to ensure that they could cover several decades of retirement, if needed. Similarly, everyone had to budget more carefully in the face of the declining economy.

Money issues were also related to the roles discussion, as it was clear that compensation had to be better tied to responsibilities and contributions. For example, Ana couldn't expect to collect consulting fees for the minimal amount of work she was doing. Similarly, no member could expect to just sit back and keep receiving dividends. Together we established some basic criteria for linking compensation to contributions, and the family started becoming more comfortable with these— and with the idea of addressing money issues directly, rather than avoiding them. This also included the extended family, where Lisa's finance-related pressure on Karl was adding to the stress. Lisa and Karl had to keep talking about money issues, but to be realistic about the economic challenges and to voice specific concerns to family members and look for solutions, rather than griping in isolation.

A final topic within this area was valuation. As transfer of ownership loomed on the horizon, especially if Sam made good on his promise to retire, the family had to agree on guidelines for assessing the business's value, as that would have affected any kind of buyout. As this was a complicated and possibly thorny issue, I suggested that the family start familiarizing themselves with ways of establishing a value (e.g., based on revenues at the time Sam officially departed versus current or future revenues) and potential issues that might come up around a buyout. It was also clear that Sam and Liz should create a comprehensive estate plan, another task they'd been avoiding.

Be real about retirement. The last topic was the "squishi-est," as it had mostly to do with personality and life circumstances, as opposed to work responsibilities or money issues. Sam and Liz had to be honest with themselves and the family about their retirement. Was it realistic for Sam to truly disengage from the business? Most signs suggested that it wasn't; the couple lacked the social and emotional resources to have a completely satisfying retirement. The point wasn't necessarily for the couple to throw in the towel on the idea, but to be more upfront with themselves and their family about what made sense for them. In short, they needed to develop a clearer long-term plan, possibly one that included Sam's maintaining a formal position with the business for some period of time before truly retiring. That would of course have led to a whole other set of questions—What should Sam's role be? How could he and Karl establish the best working relationship?—but it would have been better than the ambiguity the family faced because of Sam's straddling the line between work and retirement.

To deal with these questions, I suggested the family keep thinking and talking about them as individuals and couples, and include them on the family meeting agenda. In all of these areas, the most important values to uphold were honesty and transparency, and the Greenbergs seemed committed to doing that.

Maintaining Changes

True to their word, six months later the Greenbergs had set clearer agendas for the family meetings and begun to make real headway with defining boundaries better. For example, Sam had agreed that he would let Karl know when he wanted to come by the office, and that he wouldn't bring up issues that Karl was responsible for when he spoke to suppliers and customers. "I was undermining him without realizing it," Sam said. The family was also talking to other business families about best practices for forming a board, and Sam was excited about becoming a board member.

Ana's role had also become more clearly defined. After several tough conversations, she and Karl agreed that having her put in the consulting hours they envisioned originally was simply too stressful given her other responsibilities, and they had reduced her role accordingly—along with its associated compensation. "It's actually helped me focus on my pharmaceutical work better, and avoid having to choose between working for the business and spending time with my kids," Ana said. Martin had also become more involved with the business as discussed—he was leading a small task force to establish several college scholarships sponsored by Bob's Beds & More.

The money part was a bit more challenging. While the family had begun to discuss their goals more openly with each other, their objectives remained a bit fuzzy, which made it hard to develop a clear plan for achieving them. They also hadn't made much headway in thinking about valuation. They are not alone in this pattern; the quick decline in the economy had caught everyone by surprise, and most people were treading water, hoping to avoid another big wave of bad returns.

On the issue of Sam's retirement, there seemed to be hope. While Sam hadn't resolved to push fully into or away from retirement, he said that the past six months had helped him understand that perhaps it wasn't an "either-or" decision but one that could incorporate elements of both. "Thinking of it as flipping a switch is artificial," he said. Encouraging him to think of retirement not as the end of one phase of life but the beginning of new, more dimensional one, a stage that involved working in some capacity, relaxing more than before, and pursuing old and new interests with vigor.

In this way, we used the treatment of Boomer Retirement Mirage to help Sam gain clarity on what he wanted out of life, and for his extended family to understand how this affected their roles, responsibilities, and expectations, along with clarifying these in their own right. Even despite ongoing economic challenges, it seemed clear that the Mattress Prince's family was on their way to a more restful future.

7

My Child, My Boss

Most of the previous chapters have talked about the tricky balance business families have to strike in sharing responsibilities and finances among generations—but the stack-up symptoms so far have involved the unwillingness of older generations to part with control and money. What happens when the balance of power is on the other side, with the younger generation? What seemed unlikely in the past has become a reality for many family businesses today, as later generations start and grow businesses joined by older family members. This blend of new and old can work very well, especially when families appreciate what each member and generation brings to the table, whether skills, experience, or perspective. But for too many families the flipped roles become a source of stress and conflict, harming both the business and the family. This chapter will help families take steps to reduce that tension and harness the resources each member brings most effectively.

Balancing Foosball with Fundamentals

The interview started well enough, but went downhill quickly. Fifty-eight-year-old Mark Warren and his 28-year-old son Glen sat in a coffee shop near the home where Glen had been raised in Chicago's northern suburbs. The Warrens were talking with a reporter for a local newspaper about the business they both worked for: Warren Total Marketing (WTM). WTM had started eight years earlier, in Glen's dorm room at the University of Illinois. At the time, Glen was a junior majoring in computer science. Observing the Internet's explosive growth, he had started experimenting with Search Engine Optimization (SEO), or ways of improving traffic to a given website—still a relatively new concept then. Using his tech skills, Glen had developed several effective SEO algorithms, and begun marketing these to clients, first smaller regional businesses, then national players.

By the time Glen graduated from college, he was working nearly full-time on the business, and earning more in profits than the starting salary of any entry-level IT job he could have secured. Glen hadn't really set out to be an entrepreneur, but looking back he realized he'd always enjoyed running a business, whether mowing lawns or fixing computers in the neighborhood. Riding the wave of interest in social media and online networking, Glen expanded his services to include website development and ad-placement technologies. As a one-man shop, he found himself working longer and longer hours, often forgoing social opportunities to move projects along.

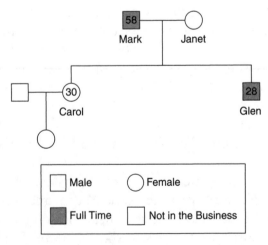

Figure 7.1 My Child, My Boss: The Warren Family

In these early years, Glen's father, Mark, an MBA and finance executive with a transportation company, supported Glen's entrepreneurship with general advice and the occasional small loan (e.g., when Glen needed to purchase new server hardware). Then Mark was laid off unexpectedly. After scrambling to find a new job and facing a bleak job market for a manager his age, Mark sat down with Glen to discuss a "radical idea": he would invest money and time to help Glen grow the business. "I believe it can be huge, son," Mark said. Within a week, the pair had agreed that Glen would be WTM's President, with Mark as CFO. "But we thought of each other as equal partners," Glen said. In fact, they decided not to use any kind of legal or financial contracts beyond those required to incorporate the business, because they "trusted" each other.

Mark's prophecy quickly came true: the business grew fast. With Mark investing a portion of the family's savings and helping Glen network with Chicago's angel investor community, WTM had the funds to lease office space in the city's West Loop and hire a set of young programmers to increase its capacity and revenues dramatically. Glen took advantage of his newly freed time (he was no longer the point person on every project) to indulge in his passion for technology, starting a blog called "Speaking Geek" and debating hardware and software issues with his staff late into the night. With a foosball table and pets-welcome policy, the office quickly took on a Silicon Valley start-up atmosphere.

The older Warren was fine with this arrangement at first. "How many of *you* can wear shorts to the office?" he asked his friends jokingly at the country club. But soon his and Glen's approaches began to clash, on more and more issues. When Glen wanted to invest in specialized programmers and greater server capacity, Mark suggested building a stronger revenue stream first. When Glen wanted to expand into larger design projects and outsource portions of the work to India or China, Mark pointed out the risks of this approach, including fluctuation in demand for such services and cultural barriers to working with overseas designers. "You don't understand new technology," Glen said to his father in frustration. "You never pay attention to fundamentals," Mark countered.

Still, father and son managed to maintain the partnership by compromising where they could and agreeing to disagree on some issues, all the while keeping any work-related issues from affecting broader family relationships. Within a year, two trends upset their uneasy alliance. First, as the market for SEO and other web-based services became increasingly commoditized, it was harder for WTM to grow. The company was forced to lay off several programmers, but its diversified and loyal customer base helped it weather the slump, as did the faith of one of its angel investors, who offered a cash infusion when bank credit became much harder to secure due to lower projected profits. Amidst this drop in business, Mark and Glen's clashes became more prominent: "Sometimes you have to spend money to make money," Glen said, to which his father just shook his head. Their conflict was also obvious at investor and other meetings, in which Mark took a "patronizing" approach, according to Glen, by treating him like a "kid" and not the successful entrepreneur he was. "I gave him a job," Glen complained, "and this is how he thanks me."

Meanwhile, Mark wasn't exactly satisfied with his son's behavior either. "It's like I had nothing to do with WTM's success," he said, speaking of Glen's frequent appearance in newspaper and online articles. According to Mark, the articles "glorified" Glen's business skills, and Glen rarely mentioned his father's role, including his significant investment in the business or his help securing angel funds. After reading several articles of this nature, Mark confronted his son, who said the omission wasn't intentional, but added that it was important "to present a young face for this kind of business." Glen also suggested that his father join him for the next interview.

Mark took his son up on the offer, which brought them to the coffeeshop near Glen's childhood home, to meet the reporter. The interview started well, with father and son joking about the challenges of working together, but it declined quickly when the reporter asked about how WTM started: Glen talked about his dorm-room enterprise, but Mark interjected that "it had really taken off" once he came on board. Glen pointed out that he could have secured outside funding without his father's help, and things escalated quickly, to the point that the interview had to be postponed. Mark and Glen continued the argument in the parking lot; in frustration, Glen said he was tempted to sell the business and start over again, alone, and Mark said Glen would be "lost" without his help.

As father and son drove away, separately, from the disastrous interview, both regretted their harsh words. But neither could think of ways to forge a healthier partnership. Each knew the other brought something valuable to the business, but they'd lost sight of one another's contributions amidst the revenue slowdown and ego bruising. Money remained a central concern; both Warrens were worried about cash flow and payroll and generating a return for investors. On top of this, Mark was concerned that working for the business might not allow him to save enough for retirement—which he hoped to make happen within the decade. Moreover, what if Glen made good on his threat to sell the business? Even with outside investors involved, there were only limited terms in place regarding ownership, and Mark cringed at the thought of a court battle with his son.

By this point the conflict had spilled over into the broader family, with the tension between father and son more obvious at the few family get-togethers they still had. Janet, Mark's wife and Glen's mother, felt she was playing the role of CEO, or "Chief Emotional Officer," always trying to maintain family harmony. "I want to support my child," she said. "But in this case that can mean going against his father." So Janet was very careful about taking sides, except in one case: her daughter, Carol, Glen's older sibling. Thirty-year-old Carol worked as an accountant and had been married for three years; she and her husband had just had their first child, a daughter. Unlike the rest of her family, Carol had been skeptical about having multiple family members in the business; in fact, she had declined to help with WTM's accounting when her father approached her about it several years ago. "I'll help you find someone, but leave me out of it," she said. "Best to keep business and family separate." Both Mark and Glen had dismissed her concerns. Now, as the tension between father and son grew, Carol felt vindicated. But it was a hollow victory. As she pointed out, the family rarely spent time together anymore, though they all lived in the Chicago area, and she was concerned that her daughter would think that her grandfather and uncle "didn't like each other." Summing up the situation, Carol said, "How can we go on like this?" Given the growing distance between Mark and Glen, it was a very good question.

My Child, My Boss: The Symptom

Fifty or even twenty years ago the idea of a parent working for his or her child may have seemed far-fetched. Today it's increasingly common. But as the Warrens found out, it often sounds better in theory than it works in practice. Manager-employee relationships always present challenges, and these are made more complicated by dual family and business roles, as in most of the previous symptoms discussed in this book (e.g., Control Beyond the Grave, Boomer Retirement Mirage). But the symptom of My Child, My Boss comes with a special twist: the reversal of roles, such that the family authority figure (i.e., the parent) takes on the subordinate business role of employee. This adds a whole other layer of complication to an already challenging relationship.

The symptom doesn't always play out the way it did for the Warrens. For example, it could be the case that a parent starts a business, then their son or daughter joins it and grows it quickly, possibly even ascending to an official position on a par with the parent's or, more likely, wielding as much or more influence over the business as the parent.

The situation's a natural breeding ground for negative emotion including entitlement, jealousy, and indignation.

Let's consider the trends that have helped drive the symptom of My Child, My Boss.

The Era of Entrepreneurship and Generational Influences

We've truly entered the Era of Entrepreneurship. Extrapolations from multiple data sets (including those of the Global Entrepreneurship Monitor) suggest that in a given year, about 472 million entrepreneurs worldwide are trying to start 305 million companies—about one-third of these are expected to be launched, meaning approximately 100 million new businesses will open annually worldwide.[1] Of course many of these are single-person shops or service businesses without much growth potential, but the number is still remarkable. The U.S. accounts for many of the new businesses, with estimates from 2005 showing about half a million new enterprises in this country per month.[2] Interestingly, the Kaufman Foundation showed that the recent rate of entrepreneurship has tended to stay constant across conditions—recessions, expansions, scarce capital, abundant capital.[3] So the recession that began in late 2007 may have daunted some individuals from starting businesses, due to low demand and availability of credit, but it inspired at least as many to go the entrepreneurial route, including those who lost corporate jobs and struggled to replace them.

More and more entrepreneurs have never worked in a corporate setting. That's especially the case with younger members of the workforce, including the younger Gen Xers and older Gen Y individuals (Millennials). Many are aiming for a better work-life balance than their parents had, and those that are self-employed report being much more satisfied with almost every aspect of their work.[4] It's a trend that's also reflected in the increasing number of entrepreneurship classes at universities.

Fast Fact

In 1985, U.S. colleges offered 250 courses on entrepreneurship; in 2009, they offered 5,000.

Source: Kira Bindrim, "College Entrepreneurship Programs Expand," *crain's new york business.com,* October 14, 2009 (http://www.crainsnewyork.com/article/20091014/SMALLBIZ/910149991) (accessed April 30, 2010).

Perhaps even more remarkable is the number of businesses that have been started on college campuses, including giants like Google, Facebook, Yahoo, and Napster, to name just a few. By some estimates, up to 70 percent of college students hope to own their own business eventually.[5] The burgeoning entrepreneurship in dorm rooms is part of the reason elite business schools like Harvard and Stanford are aiming to enroll a much higher percentage of younger students; those with significant business experience (typically entrepreneurship) before graduating can join the programs directly from college, and Harvard Business School introduced its "2+2" program in 2007, allowing college juniors to apply to the school, secure admission, and then work two years before starting.

These trends aren't surprising, given that entrepreneurs are among the biggest celebrities of the new millennium. What began with Ted Turner and Donald Trump continued with Bill Gates and Meg Whitman and Jeff Bezos and is going full-steam ahead with Jay-Z, Jerry Yang, Mark Zuckerberg, and many others. Rapper 50 Cent's 2003 album (and 2005 movie) titled "Get Rich or Die Tryin" seemed to sum up the spirit of the late Xers and Millenials as they sought to emulate these high-flyers who turned an idea into billions in revenues and personal profits. But unlike their 1980s counterparts, the new crop of starter-uppers have a wider focus than money; greed may still be good, but green is better. They're starting more socially responsible enterprises than ever before, while still turning a profit, in many cases. And having learned from the turn-of-the-millennium tech bubble and the financial meltdown of the late 2000s, they're more realistic about booms and busts, but still willing to dream big.

So where does the generational clash come in for My Child, My Boss? The table below summarizes potential points of conflict between Silent/Boomer cohorts and Gen X/ Millennials.

	Silent/Boomers	Gen X/Millennials
Professional experience	Work for someone	Work for self
Business focus	Fundamentals	Freedom
Belief in system	Rebelled against system, but bought into it	Don't believe in system
Comfort with technology	Low to medium	High to super-high
Attitude toward finances	More conservative	Willing to take risks

As the table suggests, there are multiple "flashpoints" when Boomers like Mark Warren try to work with Gen Xers or Millennials like his son Glen. Their story illustrates many of these: Mark was squarely focused on fundamentals while Glen wanted the freedom to experiment and take risks; Glen was more adept with new technology than his father; Mark had worked in the corporate world for decades, while Glen never had. In general, Mark's approach of adding structure, systems, and process clashed with Glen's focus on opportunity, flexibility, and avoiding getting locked into anything. These differences caused increasing tension and frustration for the Warrens, especially when growing WTM became more of a challenge.

Now let's consider My Child, My Boss as a potential symptom in your family business.

Diagnosing Boomer Retirement Mirage

The list below can help you think about whether your family business shows characteristics related to My Child, My Boss.

IF YOU AGREE MORE THAN DISAGREE WITH THESE STATEMENTS, MY CHILD, MY BOSS MAY BE A SYMPTOM WORTH TREATING IN YOUR FAMILY BUSINESS.

- A younger-generation member of the family started the business, serves as its "face" and visionary, and/or is responsible for much of its growth; older-generation members also work in the business.
- Disagreements about specific business issues—marketing, finances, technology, and others—occur along generational lines.
- Our company has fancy or expansive titles but lacks clarity of roles, responsibilities, and hierarchy.
- Older-generation members express dissatisfaction with the level of recognition/respect they receive for their skills and experience.
- There is dissatisfaction/disagreement regarding the "value" of money invested in business (especially by the older generation) and what constitutes a reasonable return on investment (ROI) on this money.
- There is disagreement (spoken or unspoken) about ownership of business and/or few legal documents in place stipulating ownership and other terms.
- Younger-generation siblings uninvolved in the business feel left out or that the business takes up too much of the family's time and energy.
- There are discrepant stories about who started the business and/or who deserves more credit for its growth.

Boomer Retirement Mirage: The Treatment

Families must first understand the generation-based patterns they've fallen into and why. Then practical steps are developed to alter these patterns.

Understanding the Stack-Up Patterns

After considering a series of questions about their situation (see Chapter 1), families can begin to understand their specific issues within a context, linking their challenges to underlying sources. For the Warrens, this meant highlighting the challenges associated with the roles and expectations of family members, especially as related to differences in how Mark and Glen approached business issues. As discussed above, where Mark favored a much more fundamentals-driven approach, Glen had more of a trial-and-error mentality; these reflected potential personality differences and different ages and levels of experience between father and son, but also predictable discrepancies based on the generations they came from. Their increasingly frequent disagreements about business matters and Mark's challenges related to feeling adequately recognized for his contributions had made it difficult for them to work together and disrupted the broader family's harmony. The extended family was understandably frustrated, but members like Carol weren't helping the matter by steering clear of the challenges or taking an I-told-you-so approach.

Some of the challenges the Warrens faced were a direct result of market factors—everything gets harder when business is down. At the same time, the bigger issues they had to figure out, regardless of economic conditions, involved finding a way for Mark and Glen to work together more harmoniously, if that was the solution that made the most sense for the business and the family. It was important for Glen and Mark to see that Glen's parents' support—both financial and emotional—had been a large part of his success as an entrepreneur, and that their recent conflicts had obscured some of that. The Warrens were understandably stuck in "blaming mode," which made it difficult for them to step back and see the issues they were up against—and some of the causes for these. Both Glen and Mark tended to use the content of our discussions as evidence for their individual points of view, rather than trying to gain a deeper understanding of the situation.

Once an initial understanding of the context for their issues was developed, the Warrens were able to work on changing the stack-up patterns to address the symptom of My Child, My Boss.

Changing the Stack-Up Patterns

It's not an either-or. In general, the family had failed to consider what was best for the business *and* the family, making decisions and creating conflicts that sometimes served one at the expense of the other. This was the root of many of the challenges they faced. An area in which this was a major problem was roles and responsibilities. Mark and Glen's biggest struggle was with hierarchy, as the father tried to transfer his role of authority in the family to the business, and felt threatened when the transfer didn't go well (as reflected in their many clashes over budgets and other topics). Even in a more typical family business situation, where Dad is the founder or higher-level manager, this transfer can be challenging, but it's vastly more difficult when the younger generation has founded the business or is leading it.

One way they could begin reconciling business and family was by using the family's base of strength—as exemplified by their strong relationships before the business began—as a better, ongoing resource for the business. Encouraging the family members to talk about how much interest they had taken in one another's lives and pursuits historically was important, including how well Glen's parents had supported his early entrepreneurship (e.g., lawn-mowing and tech support). Glen had forgotten how much of a role his mother's encouragement and father's advice had played in his success, seeing it as only the result of his efforts. Similarly, Glen and Mark discussed the difficult topic of who deserved "credit" for starting the business. It was clearly Glen's idea to start the business, but he'd failed to take into account how much his family's support over the years had helped him get to that point. Moreover, while Glen may have been able to secure funding without Mark's help, his father had been invaluable in connecting the business to sources of capital, and Mark's personal investment had been significant; it was important for Glen to acknowledge these contributions. At the same time, it was important for Mark not to make such a big deal of his role; more than likely, the business would have grown without his help, as valuable as it was.

With this richer shared understanding, we turned to discussing what was best for the business and the family. In order to be successful, Mark and Glen had to bring the "best of both generations" that they represented to the business. A hammer-and-nail analogy could help them think of their shared contribution to WTM : a hammer isn't of much use without a nail, and a nail can't get very far without a hammer. They needed each other, and were doing the business a disservice by clashing instead of cooperating. Glen understood the need to create and maintain a certain kind of culture for WTM, and he had great technology skills. Mark understood finances and formal decision making very well. They needed to create much better give-and-take as colleagues.

They also needed more formal systems in place on several dimensions of the business. One of these was ownership—though the business was still in its early stage, Mark and Glen had to formalize who held what part of it much better, with the anticipation that WTM would continue to grow. They also would have benefited from a more formal decision-making process, rather than deciding key issues on the fly, which lent itself easily to clashes. Part of this was about establishing a decision-making system that involved making a clear business case for recommendations large and small, and pulling in other colleagues to weigh in as needed. Yes, such a system might diminish some of WTM's freewheeling atmosphere, but that environment had stimulated too many conflicts already; in the future they might reach a better balance between formal and informal. Another step involved creating and using advisory boards to help in decision making, and creating a formal board of directors once WTM was large enough. To facilitate the process, the family met weekly in a location away from the office to discuss these issues.

Regarding the family, Mark and Glen were urged to take into account how much their business-related issues were affecting everyone. The more specific steps discussed fell mostly into the next category of general advice.

Make it an "all play." It was critical for the broader family (i.e., mother Janet, sister Carol, and Carol's family) to understand that in a family business situation everyone is involved, whether they want to be or not. In this context, most of the time it was fine for Janet to be the Chief Emotional Officer—it was a natural role for her, and one she played effectively—but she sometimes had to be clearer about "taking sides" (which I urged her to see as helping in decision-making, rather than making an emotional statement). She also had to be more vocal about her concerns and wishes for the business and family; expressing herself more would help Mark and Glen take the family into account better, and manage their conflicts accordingly.

It was also important that Carol stop taking herself out of the situation with blanket statements about not mixing business with family. In the Warrens' case, it was too late; they were a business family, and now they had to deal with it actively. This didn't mean that Carol had to join the business; it was perfectly reasonable that she continue working outside of it—if anything, this helped balance the family's priorities. But it did mean that she should communicate her specific feelings about the business's effects, especially the conflicts between Glen and Mark, more thoroughly. They may not have been able to avail themselves of Carol's talents as an accountant, but they needed her to help keep the family emotionally healthy. For example, she had to take more of a role in making family decisions that might affect the business, such as spending time together or making financial decisions.

To promote all of these changes, the family began to use formal family meetings with clear agendas to discuss business and family issues. They could no longer deny that the business affected the family and vice versa, and such meetings would provide a forum for discussing these. The meetings would also be an important foundation for handling important issues, including those related to money and retirement, once the business grew.

Manage ego issues. Many of the Warrens' conflicts arose over who deserved more credit for starting and growing the business. The reality, of course, was that *both* father and son had a hand in WTM's success (as did Janet and Carol). Given that, we examined the factors making this a frequent point of contention. The biggest one was Mark's need to preserve a sense of success and self-worth. Having been laid off late in his successful career as a manager, he had little to hang his proverbial hat on, and it was natural for him to seek recognition for his role in WTM. He also admitted privately to me that as tensions between him and Glen had grown, he had been occasionally checking online classifieds for other opportunities, though he was committed to staying with WTM in general.

The three of us discussed how best to reconcile their stories about how WTM had started and what/who had promoted its success. We talked about the idea of "licensing" different stories for different settings, including business, social, and other contexts. And they had to be unified in their approach. For example, while it might have been okay for Mark to overstate his role a bit over cocktails with friends at the country club, this wasn't appropriate for newspaper interviews, which required a more balanced telling of the story, and maybe one that even overemphasized the "young entrepreneur" angle, as this might help gain more publicity for WTM.

This was a tough conversation for the Warrens to have, given the history of conflict over this issue. But they agreed to talk through it and try to find a mutually agreeable solution.

Maintaining Changes

Several months later, the Warrens reported some positive changes, including with regard to being more mindful of what was best for both the business and the family. For one, they had started what they called "Reconnection Dinners," monthly meals the extended family shared to keep their bonds strong. At these dinners, business talk was discouraged, but not prohibited; rather, they focused on catching up on personal matters and enjoying time with Carol's daughter. They were also using regular family meetings to discuss business issues, including the effects of the recession on WTM. "The meetings really help us understand business issues through the lens of the family," Mark said. Carol mentioned that she recognized for the first time that her hands-off approach had been detrimental to family harmony, and the family reported that she was a very active contributor to family-meeting discussions.

With regard to doing what was best for the business, Glen and Mark said that they had drawn clearer lines between their responsibilities, with accounting and general financials (e.g., dealing with the credit market) as Mark's domain, product development and marketing as Glen's arena, and shared responsibility for investment decisions and meetings with investors. They agreed that presenting a unified face to investors, customers, and partners was paramount and said that they had been "much better" with this overall. They had also taken steps toward putting more formal contracts in place, including meeting with attorneys to discuss key issues. Partly because of this progress, WTM had been weathering the downturn much better than some of its competitors.

Mark and Glen had had a tougher time taking my advice of reconciling their stories of the business better. Each still tended to overemphasize his role in building WTM, and discussions of this issue tended not to go well. Mark and Glen agreed that they should stay away from joint interviews for the time being, and that Glen should make it a point to mention his father's role when he did speak to the media at any length.

Overall, the Warrens seemed highly satisfied with their progress with WTM and as a family. They were approaching the business with an open, unified approach, more like what they'd enjoyed back when Glen mowed lawns and fixed computers in the neighborhood.

8

Generation-Straddling Siblings

The previous chapters discussed the challenges business families face when multiple generations work together. But what happens when age differences among a set of siblings place its members so far apart that they've effectively been raised in different generational contexts? That's becoming more and more frequent for business families, given trends and technology related to birth patterns, as well as the rising rates of remarriage and blended families. The result is a new layer of stack-up-related complications: generation-based conflicts among siblings, rather than between parents and children. The challenge is that siblings often have less clearly defined roles—and much more potential for jealousy—than parents and children do, making for conflicts that are more difficult to resolve in many cases. This chapter helps families understand the sources and nature of these points of conflict, and take practical steps to overcome them.

A Tale of Three Houses

When Ted Tompkins was born, the entire family was excited. "A surprise gift," his parents Steve and Sheila called the baby when they brought him back to their home in the Maryland suburbs of Washington, DC. The "surprise" part was that the couple thought their family was already complete: son Dan was

18 and heading to college; daughter Cindy was 10, a fourth-grader. And there was even a third "sibling": Tompkins Jet, a jet parts manufacturing company Steve, an aviation engineer, had launched five years before Ted was born. Ted's birth was good timing, as the business had just become profitable, after a long period of hard work and uncertainty.

Over the next decades the children grew, along with the business. Elder son Dan had been excited about joining Tompkins Jet since his teenage years, when the business first started. Dan helped out with office work part-time while in high school, and learned from his father the many challenges of early-stage entrepreneurship. "No risk, no reward," Steve often said in those early years. The unspoken question then was, "How long until the reward?" For capital, Steve and Sheila had taken out a large second mortgage and borrowed from friends, families, and banks. Name-brand foods disappeared from their cupboards, they skipped vacations, and rarely even went out to the movies. As he finished high school, Dan felt the belt-tightening in bigger ways: a star baseball player, he earned a partial athletic scholarship to an out-of-state private school, but had to attend a large public in-state university to minimize expenses. Never wavering in his interest in working for Tompkins Jet, Dan interned with the company every summer and joined as an operations analyst right out of college. A hard worker, he advanced steadily, taking on more responsibility as the business grew.

By the time middle child, Cindy, reached high school, Tompkins Jet was on a major upswing, having diversified into several niche markets for airplane parts within a fast-growing airline industry. Partly to make up for the lean years they had endured while building the business, Steve and Sheila moved their family into a large home in a more upscale neighborhood. Cindy invited friends over for weekend pool parties and bought as many designer clothes as her large closet could hold. When she secured admission to the same out-of-state college Dan had been forced to decline, there was no question that she could go, and she did, also enjoying a semester in Spain.

Cindy took pre-law courses and decided to postpone law school to work in advertising. "Maybe you can help Tompkins Jet with marketing," Steve said. Cindy told her father she'd consider it, but that her heart was still set on law. "We can always use good lawyers," Steve said. Three years later, Cindy earned her JD, then got married the year after she graduated, deciding to take time off from her busy corporate attorney position when she became pregnant with her first child. Five years and another child later, Cindy, by then in her mid-thirties, was ready to return to work. But she wanted more flexibility than a corporate law position would allow; working with the family business seemed much more appealing now. After discussing options with Steve, Cindy joined Tompkins Jet as a part-time legal consultant. Dan expressed initial concern that the position's flexibility might lead to "commitment issues" on Cindy's part, but he ultimately agreed that she should join.

Unlike his siblings, Ted had no memories of the family's challenging financial circumstances. He was three years old when they moved to their second home, and by the time he finished elementary school, they'd moved to an even more luxurious residence, in a gated community. Tompkins Jet had continued to grow, including by winning lucrative government contracts. Given his distance in age from his siblings, Ted was raised more like an only child, and a very privileged one: where Dan and Cindy had attended the large public high school in their district, Ted went to an exclusive private school with only 20 students in each grade; Dan had learned baseball on community center fields, but Ted honed his tennis and golf skills with private coaching at their country club; Cindy had been ecstatic to spend a college semester in Spain, while Ted took overseas trips with family and friends for granted, spending two college summers crisscrossing Europe. Ted earned a tennis scholarship to a small East Coast college, but stopped playing for the team his sophomore year, because he "lost interest."

During college, Ted spent one summer as a marketing intern for Tompkins Jet. "If he'd been anyone else, he would've been fired," Dan said, recalling how his brother repeatedly showed up late for work and turned in low-quality deliverables. The problem didn't seem to be with Ted's capabilities (e.g., he always scored well on standardized tests like the SAT), but with his motivation. After college, Ted worked for two years as a copywriter for a New York advertising agency, then moved to Los Angeles to pursue screenwriting. "This way he'll find the best career for him," Steve said when Dan hinted that continuing to help Ted with living expenses may not have been ideal.

After 18 months in LA, Ted worked as a ski instructor in Colorado until he suffered a knee injury that required him to take a less physically taxing position. Now in his late twenties, Ted asked to join the family business, and stepped into a marketing position. With little savings, he lived at home in the large guesthouse at the back of the property. At Tompkins Jet, Ted's work showed glimpses of great promise, but he struggled to make deadlines and attend meetings. Nonetheless, within two years Steve moved him into a marketing director position with several direct reports. Though earning a generous salary, Ted opted to continue living at home, because it was "easier."

By then Dan was in his late forties. As expected, he had risen quickly in the business, to the point where he was head of manufacturing. Other senior managers, including his father, Steve, who was fast approaching retirement, saw Dan as the best successor for the CEO position—he'd spent nearly three decades with the business, and was respected as a hard worker and "straight-shooter." Dan had been married for 20 years and had three teenage children. His sister Cindy had continued splitting her time between working at the business as a legal consultant and shuttling her two children from school to sports and other activities.

Though the siblings generally got along, negative feelings were rising among them. Each believed the others might be looking out primarily for their own best interests: Dan was seen as focused only on taking over the business; Cindy was viewed as trying to "have it all," sometimes at the expense

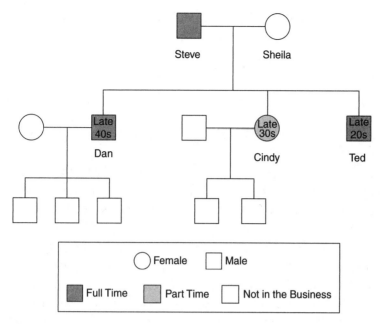

Figure 8.1 Generation-Straddling Siblings: The Tompkins Family

of the business; both Dan and Cindy felt that Ted was taking advantage of their parents' patience and generosity. Depending on the issue—from compensation to time spent on the job to performance—two of the siblings would gang up on the third, or each would raise issues independently, forcing the others to defend their opinions and actions. Steve and Sheila observed these disputes with dismay, saying, "We want to support each of you in the way that's best for you." Dan suggested that their approach "wasn't the best for the business," and hinted that things would change when he was in charge. This bothered his parents deeply, as they felt he might even oust one or both of his siblings in the future. They'd discussed formalizing a family constitution that would prohibit this, but "hadn't gotten around to it," partly because they knew how much conflict the process might cause. When it was just the two of them, Steve and Sheila reminisced wistfully about how much easier life had seemed when Ted was first born—they'd lived in a much smaller house, but the business had finally become profitable, the two older siblings were happy, and it was hard to imagine ever having the depth of family conflict that had now become routine.

Generation-Straddling Siblings: The Symptom

Bigger isn't always better. The Tompkins family discovered this firsthand; as their family and business grew, they faced new challenges on multiple levels, issues that made them yearn for simpler times. As many family businesses find out, the sibling stage of the business can be confusing and frustrating, as brothers and sisters struggle to find a place in the company, bringing distinct skills and preferences and historical relationship patterns to the business setting. This is hard even when siblings are close enough in age to be considered from the same generation. It can be even more challenging when siblings are far apart age-wise, to the point that they're squarely in different generations. On the one hand, such siblings may have fewer relationship-based issues (e.g., rivalry), because they didn't engage much with each other growing up or overlap in school and other arenas like sports. On the other hand, they've often been raised in very different circumstances, as the Tompkinses' three different homes illustrate. In addition, they're subject to varying generation-based influences that may result in clashing perspectives on things such as performance expectations and work-life balance. Dan, Cindy, and Ted represented Boomers, Gen X, and Gen Y, respectively. That's what makes Generation-Straddling Siblings such a potent symptom: you're often dealing with issues that stem from a combination of (1) underlying sibling relationships, (2) highly different family experiences for each sibling, and (3) generation-based patterns and conflicts. And the whole thing gets more complicated when you add a remarriage or blended-family situation to the mix (as was the case for the Brown family in the Introduction chapter).

Let's consider the trends that have helped drive the symptom of Generation-Straddling Siblings.

Birth-Related Trends, Blended Families, and Generational Clashes

Worldwide greater longevity, the advancement and availability of birth control and reproductive technologies, and the postponement of motherhood for educational and career opportunities is enabling women to prolong their fertility an unprecedented number of years. There is a much larger window in which many women can give birth, one that's over three decades now—from teen years to middle or even late forties. That of course means older parents than before, but also wider average gaps between children. Though statistics are hard to find, there's a lot of anecdotal evidence for larger gaps between children.

Another trend that contributes to the longer gaps between children is the rising number of blended families, where one or both parents have children from a previous relationship. What seemed unique when the TV show *The Brady Bunch* debuted in the 1970s (i.e., the marriage of two previously married people who both bring children to the union) is now commonplace. Up-to-date statistics for U.S. rates of blended families are hard to find, partly because the U.S. Census stopped providing estimates of marriage, divorce, and remarriage in 1990. The 1990 census estimated that 50 percent of U.S. children lived with a stepparent (which fits well with the generally accepted statistic of a 50 percent divorce rate).[1]

Fast Fact

By the year 2000, there were estimated to be more step- or blended families than traditional families.

Source: *Stepfamily.org*, quoting 1990 U.S. Census (http://www.stepfamily.org/statistics.html) (accessed May 6, 2010).

While blended families have become the norm today, it's important to remember that they often introduce new dimensions of challenge that traditional families don't face. Here the Brady Bunch depiction of a blended family fails to mirror reality, given that the TV family acts more or less like a traditional one.[2] In reality, alliances and conflicts tend to occur along bloodlines in blended families, and these can be intensified by a family business situation. Having siblings with different sets of parents ("yours, my, and our" children) and wide gaps between them in a blended business family adds even more complexity to the situation, again as illustrated by the Brown family in the first chapter. Note that elements of the Generation-Straddling Siblings symptom can also appear in family business situations where multiple cousins with large age gaps work together.

Finally, birth order, the distinct family contexts (e.g., economic status) experienced by each child, and generational differences all play a role in the symptom of Generation-Straddling Siblings. Experts in psychology and other fields disagree on the specific effects of birth order, with studies linking it to personality, intelligence, sexuality, and other characteristics. One prominent researcher argues that first-born children are likely to be more conscientious and dominant, but less open to new ideas than their siblings; some studies support this claim.[3] This pattern occurred in the Tompkins family, with the eldest sibling, Dan, the most hard-working of the three.

Family context was likely of greater influence on the Tompkins children than birth order, though these two factors are clearly linked in this example. While Dan grew up in a situation marked by financial uncertainty and lots of sacrifices, Cindy split her childhood years between a modest lifestyle and one of greater luxury, and Ted enjoyed a very privileged life including private schools and frequent trips abroad. These very different experiences can—and did, in this case—lead to perceptions of unfairness among siblings. Dan felt that he had worked hard for things his siblings had taken for granted (e.g., college and a position with the business), and Ted felt that any success he achieved would be discounted because he'd been "handed" everything. As the middle child—and the only female—Cindy often felt overlooked, largely because her siblings' issues tended to trump her own. These patterns, related to early family experiences, were also present in their work relationships, and their issues at work further affected their family relationships.

On top of birth order and family-context influences, the Tompkins siblings were subject to generation-based differences. Given the wide age-spacing among them and the short duration of Gen X births, each was effectively raised in a different generation: Dan was a young Boomer, Cindy was squarely within Gen X, and Ted was an older Gen Y member, or Millennial. How did these cohort memberships affect their outlooks and actions? Like many Boomers, Dan had more of an "old-school" approach to work and family: you went to school, started your career, committed yourself to one company (the family business, in this case), then got married and started a family. Cindy faced a major challenge many Gen Xers face: work-life balance. She had one foot in her work responsibilities, one foot in active motherhood, and a "third" foot in her own pursuits, including teaching yoga. In pursuing each of these, she embodied elements of the symptom of Comfortable Gen X, which I discuss in more detail in the next chapter. Finally, Ted, like many Millennials, had received deep support from his parents (including their financial resources) in everything from academics to athletics. He had the luxury of pursuing multiple career paths—advertising, screenwriting, ski instruction, and finally the family business—without really having to commit to any one of them. In fact, he arguably never wanted to be in the family business but ultimately felt he "had to be," due to circumstance and capability. Partly as a result of his situation he hadn't gained the management skills he needed to perform well in the position to which he was promoted. Naturally, these very different perspectives and expectations caused clashes among the Tompkins siblings, without their recognizing their grounding in generational differences.

Now let's consider Generation-Straddling Siblings as a potential symptom in your family business.

Diagnosing the Symptom of
Generation-Straddling Siblings

The list below can help you think about whether your family business shows characteristics related to Generation-Straddling Siblings.

IF YOU AGREE MORE THAN DISAGREE WITH THESE STATEMENTS, GENERATION-STRADDLING SIBLINGS MAY BE A SYMPTOM WORTH TREATING IN YOUR FAMILY BUSINESS.

- Some of the siblings (or cousins) working in our family business have large age gaps (i.e., at least eight to ten years) between them.
- There are significant perceptions of unfairness among the siblings involved in our family business.
- The siblings in our family business who are more than four years apart don't spend much time together outside of work.
- The parent generation of the family business deals with each sibling in very different ways (i.e., expectations, support through money or other means).
- Siblings in our family business grew up in different family contexts—as related to finances, parents' presence, and other factors.
- There is a significant lack of trust among siblings in our family business.
- There is significant conflict among siblings over responsibilities, advancement within the business, compensation, succession, and related issues.
- There is significant conflict regarding siblings' work ethic and level of commitment to the business in general.
- There is significant jealousy over past events or patterns within the family (and this affects work relationships).

Generation-Straddling Siblings: The Treatment

Families must first understand the generation-based patterns they've fallen into and why. Practical steps are then developed to alter these patterns.

Understanding the Stack-Up Patterns

After considering a series of questions about their situation (see Chapter 1), families can begin to understand their specific issues within a context, linking their challenges to underlying sources. In the case of the Tompkins family, there was no way the siblings could escape the legacy of the significant shifts in their family's fortunes: Dan, Cindy, and Ted had grown up in very different "worlds," with the difference most pronounced between Dan and Ted. Their generational memberships only compounded these differences.

The family had to work to accept that these differences weren't going to go away, but that they could manage the expectations and negative emotions associated with them more effectively. One exercise that helped the Tompkins family was what I call "Remember When." I asked the family to remember when they'd all been living under the same roof, and what their lives and relationships were like. For the siblings, this meant the period when Dan was 18 and heading off to college, Cindy was 10 and in fourth grade, and Ted had just been born. Most families carry the way they related when they last lived together into their adult relationships— for better *and* worse. Therefore the approaching responsibilities that Dan faced as a young man starting college (under difficult financial circumstances) had carried into the hard work he did at the family business; Cindy's busy life as a fourth-grader (with focus on multiple areas) mirrored that of her adult life as a mother, professional, and yoga instructor; Ted's having everything done for him as a baby paralleled that of his young adulthood. And their adult relationships with one another reflected this history as well. The family was able to use the exercise not as a way of forcing themselves to accept the way things were, but to understand the sources of their challenges and to begin working to address them.

Changing the Stack-Up Patterns

My suggestions to the Tompkins family involved several mutually reinforcing categories of advice.

Tame the green-eyed monster. Jealousy is inevitable in families, and a major challenge in many family businesses. The problem is that many people, including in business families, don't admit their envy—even to themselves—then are puzzled when they feel its negative effects. The Tompkins family had all kinds of issues related to jealousy, some that they realized and voiced, and some that they did not. As an early step, we worked to have each sibling talk about what they envied about the others, partly by linking their feelings to the "Remember When" exercise mentioned above. This was easiest for Dan; he'd already made clear that he believed he'd had to work for everything that was handed to his siblings—from college tuition to a position in the business. Cindy talked about feeling overlooked as the middle child and only girl, especially when there was conflict between her brothers. Ted surprised both of his siblings by talking about how he envied them—Dan for his work ethic and having earned everything he'd achieved, and Cindy for having such a full life. Ted acknowledged that he felt like a "failure," given his multiple careers; worse, he felt that even when he did achieve something, it was seen as the result of his privileged position, rather than his efforts.

From acknowledgment we moved into mitigation. Each sibling needed to focus on the benefits of their positions in the family and the business: Dan had earned great responsibility and a high-profile position as his father's likely successor; Cindy led a "dream life" for a Gen Xer, with responsibilities at work, at home, and for her own pursuits; Ted was still young enough to make major career shifts if he chose to, and had family support for this, both emotionally and financially. To diminish perceptions of unfairness at work, the family needed to create better transparency and accountability (e.g., clear goals and criteria for achieving these) for each sibling. Finally, I reminded them that some feelings of envy would likely persist, but through better communication and perspective, these would be much more manageable.

Use strengths of differences. Historically, the family had only clashed about their differences—including those related to generational membership—rather than celebrating them. It was easier to see the potential for this shift at Tompkins Jet, where each sibling brought unique strengths. Dan had been a high-performer based on his focus on fundamentals and ability to build a strong network within the company and outside of it. Cindy had achieved a level of work-life balance that helped her feel satisfied about each of her roles and perform well within them. Ted brought creativity and a fresh perspective to the business, including knowledge of storytelling and digital marketing as powerful promotion tools. Acknowledging these strengths for themselves and one another helped the family keep thinking about how to use them to drive business benefits.

Individual strengths could also be part of improving family relationships. In this context, Cindy needed to help Dan with work-life balance, something he'd struggled with quietly for years. And Dan and Cindy needed to help Ted to take more responsibility for his work and home lives. Ted admitted that he "felt bad" about living at home, but that he was reluctant to move out because he wasn't sure about his career. We talked about the underpinnings for this fear but mostly about how it was holding him back from being accountable and making career progress. He agreed to set a goal of moving out within a year. In this regard Steve and Sheila, the parents, had to be very careful about undermining Ted's progress, even unconsciously. They were so accustomed to providing their younger children whatever they needed—partly to make up for the difficult years they'd faced before the business became profitable—that they had made it a challenge for Ted to take responsibility for his own life. Moreover, Sheila's babying of Ted was causing tension between her and Steve and making it harder for Ted to become independent.

Come together. In a sense, this was the overarching theme of my work with the Tompkins family, and with many others: they had to come together in multiple ways, at work and at home. While they felt that they still communicated, it was largely indirect (i.e., triangulating, as discussed in the Control beyond the Grave chapter) and often to voice complaints. Sharing their feelings of envy and the bases for these was a good first step, but the Tompkins siblings had to become much more diligent about discussing topics—even difficult ones—in formal and informal settings. Developing a comprehensive family constitution including a code of conduct, rights and responsibilities, and rules of engagement was an important step that Steve and Sheila had been avoiding, due to the potential conflict associated with it. By taking small steps and establishing minor, less controversial guidelines first, the family could work up to more difficult areas such as succession and rules for joining and staying in the business. The constitution is critical for the next generation—there were already five members of the third generation, and some of them might eventually want to join the business. Having clear thinking and processes in place for this would help prevent conflicts for the next Tompkins cohort. Learning from other family businesses that had created a constitution would also be beneficial to the Tompkins clan.

Maintaining Changes

Perhaps the best news was that the Tompkins family's overall level of jealousy went down dramatically during the next several months. This was largely due to their continuing to be open with one another about multiple topics. "It was hard at first," Dan said, "but it got easier." For example, Dan had been able to talk more openly about his concerns regarding Ted's performance as a manager—he had discussed some of these with Ted for the first time, rather than complaining to their father behind Ted's back. Ted had admitted that he felt poorly equipped to handle some of his responsibilities, and they'd discussed how to make sure he continued to improve his skills without impeding his team or the broader business. The family had agreed to send Ted (and Dan) to a two-week executive training program at a major business school. Dan, Steve, and Ted had also established better accountability for Ted, agreeing on specific goals and creating a "put-your-hand-up" policy that would prevent any of them from avoiding discussions; they had to ask for help as needed, moving them from a model of dependence to independence to interdependence.

The family had also made progress on leveraging the strengths of their differences. For the first time, Ted was excited about using his skills to advance the business: he had asked to handle development of the company's new website. Cindy was pleased that her siblings looked to her for advice on work-life balance—Dan with regard to juggling professional and family responsibilities, and Ted with regard to thinking about his dating life, which hadn't been going well. Dan also felt that his siblings saw him as a mentor at work for the first time, as both Cindy and Ted had approached him for advice on some of their responsibilities at Tompkins Jet.

Overall, the family meetings had helped both generations talk about issues large and small and spend time enjoying each other's company as adults for the first time. Their Sunday night dinners had become much more pleasant as well. Steve admitted that he'd continued to drag his feet on developing a constitution, partly because "things were going so well" that he was worried about disrupting their harmony. Ted mentioned that he'd still been "reluctant" about making plans to move out of the family home. I knew that the Tompkinses still had a lot of work to do, but felt they were better equipped than ever to do it. Moreover, I knew that they once again viewed the wide gaps between the siblings as a "gift," rather than focusing on the many challenges associated with these for the family and their business.

9

Comfortable Gen X

It used to be that we worked too hard. In the fast growth of the 1980s and 1990s, long hours at the office became a badge of commitment to the company, one often associated with promotions and other perks. People, especially men, routinely chose career over time with family and friends, and job responsibilities over hobbies. Such workaholism is still alive and well in many quarters of the United States and other countries—careers like banking and consulting are notorious for their combination of high compensation and challenging lifestyles. But there has been a growing backlash to the notion of "live to work," and today many professionals have turned that phrase on its head: they work to live, enjoying multiple aspects of life outside the office. This has become a hallmark characteristic of Gen X. Their quest for balance is admirable, and has resulted in many benefits like higher quality family time and better physical fitness (for some of us). But it also creates challenges; when work responsibilities take a back seat to other pursuits, productivity can suffer, and tension regarding roles and responsibilities can arise. In family businesses, the issues can be even more complicated, as there are often fewer "hands on deck," meaning that the unavailability of any given person causes bigger problems; moreover, different generations often have very different perspectives on work-life balance, resulting in clashes. In this chapter we explore the consequences of Gen X's ongoing quest for "comfort," and how to handle these in a family business.

Where's Jay?

The most common question around the office at P.K. Construction wasn't about profitability, customer relationships, or marketing strategy. It was "Where's Jay?" Managers asked this when they saw the empty seat at weekly meetings. Employees asked it on job sites when they had an important question that was holding up the work. Customers asked it when they called P.K.'s offices.

The answer wasn't always the same. Sometimes Jay was out to lunch with customers, prospects, or colleagues—especially the coworkers he'd hired from among his friends. Sometimes Jay had left early to help coach his kids' sports teams. Sometimes he was at a music event or extended family get-together. Sometimes no one knew where Jay was. While this situation would have been a problem for any P.K. Construction employee, it was an especially difficult problem in Jay King's case because of his position in the company and the family that owned it: he was general manager, and son of the founder.

Jay, 41 years old, headed operations for the construction firm his father, Paul King, had launched 15 years earlier in Phoenix, Arizona. It was Paul's second attempt at entrepreneurship; his first company, a machine-tool manufacturing one, had failed when Jay was in college. P.K. Construction specialized in building apartment complexes and had enjoyed steady growth for most of its lifetime, as demand for residential housing rose for much of the 2000s.

Jay had worked with his father's company for nearly a decade. Although he could have joined P.K. after graduating from college, he chose not to, partly because he'd observed the challenges his father faced with his first business. Still, Jay had worked in a related field: mortgage banking. Like construction, the industry was growing rapidly, and Jay was good at it, easily navigating both spreadsheets and customer relationships. He was promoted twice at the bank, and eventually left to earn an MBA.

As Jay finished business school, Paul approached him about joining P.K. "Business is booming, son," he said, "and we could use your help." Jay thought about it for a few days, then took his father up on the offer. Will, his younger brother, also joined the company at the time, in an operations role. Jay became a finance manager; at first he thrived at the job, showing up early at the office, leading multiple meetings, and going with his father to important customer events. Everyone agreed that Jay's arrival had boosted business and contributed to a high-energy atmosphere.

The problems started soon after Jay married Carolina, his on-again, off-again girlfriend who had been his coworker at the bank. Carolina was the oldest first-generation daughter of a large family that had emigrated from Mexico. She and Jay enjoyed many holidays and other cultural events with her family, even traveling to Mexico for extended family visits. When Jay and Carolina had their first child, a son—followed by a daughter fourteen months later—both families were overjoyed. Carolina's family wanted to see the children as much as possible, both on weekends and during the week. Carolina had stopped working at the bank when she became pregnant with their son.

Even before the children were born, Carolina's favorite statement to her husband was "You work too hard." She knew Jay was passionate about his work for the family business, but wanted to make sure he was available for her, her family, and, ultimately, the children. At her urging, Jay began missing some evening and weekend events, including golf outings with key customers. Jay was also enthusiastic about coaching his children's soccer and baseball teams—the kids were ten and nine by then, with weekly games and practices. Jay was pleased that the flexibility of his role with the family business allowed him to take part.

Carolina also reminded Jay about his other passion: blues music. An avid guitarist since high school, Jay played in

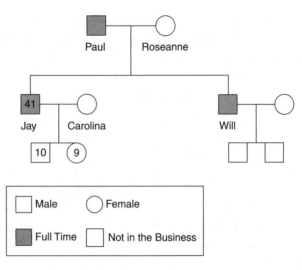

Figure 9.1   Comfortable Gen X: The King Family

bands and went to concerts regularly. But he did little of that when he first joined P.K. Two years ago, Carolina encouraged him to pick up his interest again, and soon Jay even agreed to help run a large blues music festival in Phoenix. The festival involved months of preparation and intense work for the week that it ran, time that often took Jay away from his responsibilities at P.K. He'd also recruited several friends—managers he'd hired for P.K.—to help with the festival, so the impact on the company was even greater.

At first, Paul King had been supportive of his son's pursuits outside work, largely due to the encouragement of Roseanne, his wife. And Jay's unavailability had been less of an issue initially, because it was limited and the business had continued to grow steadily. But as Jay's responsibilities grew, his absences became more frequent, and as demand for construction dropped rapidly starting in 2008, Paul expressed his concern to his son. "You gave up everything for work, Dad," Jay said, reminding Paul how little he'd been present in Jay's teenage years, as he tried to build his first business. "I'm not going to do that." Though Jay was adamant about maintaining his flexibility, he wasn't willing to give up any of the other benefits of working for the family business. When Paul suggested Jay consider a salary cut, which most managers had already agreed to, Jay was resistant, pointing out that he had to worry about paying for two college educations. In fact, Carolina was pushing for Jay to ask for more money, because he "brought so much business" to P.K (something that hadn't been true for years). Meanwhile, Jay's brother, Will, whose two children were several years younger than Jay's, complained to his parents that Jay's lack of commitment "set a bad example" for other employees and that giving him so much flexibility "wasn't fair."

The trouble with Jay came to a head when Paul asked him to handle laying off several managers he'd hired, due to declining demand. "Dad," Jay protested, "these are my friends we're talking about." Still, he agreed to take care of it within two weeks. When that date came and went, Paul confronted Jay, who said he "hadn't gotten around to it yet." By then Jay had become busier preparing for the blues festival, and "Where's Jay?" was an often-asked question. After another week passed, Paul called Jay into his office and demanded an explanation. Jay remained silent, and Paul couldn't contain his anger any longer; he berated Jay about his lack of commitment to the company and how much he'd taken Paul's support for granted. "You're going to have to choose between P.K. and everything else," Paul said. The uncertainty in Jay's eyes suggested that he didn't feel equipped to make this choice, and that if he were forced to, it wasn't clear which he would choose.

Comfortable Gen X: The Symptom

Many of us dream of combining a job we love with the flexibility to spend time with family and pursue fitness and other interests—without giving up income or opportunities for advancement. For most of us, this remains a pipedream: we face inevitable trade-offs, giving up flexibility for money, or vice versa. Yet some of us manage to create and maintain a tricky balance of finances and freedom. The odds of pulling this off seem better for business families, as members employed in the business can set their own schedules and often enjoy enviable stability compared to those in typical corporate jobs. But as the King family example illustrates, freedom has its downside. The problem is that staying productive in a family-business position requires a certain measure of self-policing, because it may take a lot to get fired when you're working for Mom or Dad or your uncle. This has been a long-standing problem for business families, but it has been exacerbated by the advancement of Generation X to management positions. Why? Because Gen Xers, more than any previous cohort, face greater challenges figuring out who they are—and where career fits into that equation. I've named this symptom Comfortable Gen X because it seems like Gen X has it all: career, family, and other interests ranging from travel to music to spiritual healing. But the reality is that at the core of all this "comfort" is confusion about where Gen X's priorities should lie. And that causes a lot of *discomfort* for family businesses with Gen Xers in important positions.

Let's consider the trends that have helped drive the symptom of Comfortable Gen X.

The Struggles of the Self-Esteem Generation

In the case of Gen X, "X" marks the spot between two huge generations. Gen Xers (an estimated 45 million people) were born in the 15 years between the longer birth periods of the Boomers (estimated at about 75 million in number) and the Millennials (at least 75 million).[1] So, in a sense, by being sandwiched between two larger groups, Gen X was "set up" to struggle with creating a niche and identity for itself, like a middle child with two very dynamic siblings. Any such struggle was intensified by Gen X's collective

early experience, which included the crumbling of traditional institutions like the Soviet Union, the mall, and the
lifelong job. As children, Gen Xers watched the rise of
downsizing; as adults, they fell victim to it. Such trends
contributed to a dubious honor for Gen X men: they became
the first generation that failed to surpass their fathers in
average income, according to a recent large-scale economic
study.[2]

Fast Fact

In 2004, Gen X men made an estimated 12 percent less than
their fathers did at the same age.

Source: Economic Mobility Project, "Economic Mobility in
America: Is the American Dream Alive and Well?" July 2008
(http://www.economicmobility.org/reports_and_research/
other?id=0003) (accessed May 18, 2010).

Moreover, Generation X inherited the now-crumbling infrastructure of the Boomers and earlier cohorts: investment
banks with household names like Bear Stearns and Lehman
Brothers, along with big-box retailers like Circuit City,
are dead and gone; American icon Anheuser Busch brew-
ing company (makers of Budweiser beer) is now owned by
Belgian company InBev.

With these changes have gone many of the entry-level
management jobs easily stepped into by generations before
Gen X. As a result, one of the hardest-hit segments of
Gen X is its youngest: those born between 1975 and 1980.
For example, in late 2009, newly minted MBAs (average age
around 30), faced a dismal job market, due to the ongoing
global recession—79 percent of business schools reported a
decline in recruiting for 2009, the same as for the previous
year.[3] And when people do manage to land jobs, they tend
to stay in them for less time than before: a 2008 study found
that average tenure in previous and current positions for the
55-to-64-year age group was 9.9 years, whereas for the 24-to-
34-year group (predominantly Gen X), it was 2.7 years.[4]

Such shifts have made Gen X members much less likely to stake their identity on their job. But that's not just because they're having trouble finding or staying in jobs. It's also the result of a backlash against the workaholism of the 1980s, 1990s, and tech boom. Sure, there will always be those who work too much, but more and more people and groups have been calling for limits to work, like the organizers of Seattle's "Take Back Your Time," who advocated for a mandatory three weeks of time off and overtime caps in 2004.[5]

You can see these Gen-X-related trends as part of a broader struggle to find sources of personal validation other than work or even family. As discussed in the Meet the MEOWs chapter, this is a generation that witnessed a tripling in the divorce rate.[6] So perhaps it's not surprising that Generation X was the first cohort to embrace the popularity of "daily affirmations," or positive self-statements people could repeat daily to feel good about themselves. The paragon of daily affirmations was Stuart Smalley, a *Saturday Night Live* character played by now-Senator Al Franken; sitting in front of a mirror in his powder blue cardigan and yellow button-down, Smalley would tell himself things like, "I'm good enough, I'm smart enough, and doggone it, people like me!" While most Gen Xers probably aren't using daily affirmations—or wearing powder blue cardigans (anymore)—many share Smalley's sentiment. That is, this "self-esteem generation" seeks multiple sources of validation, but doesn't always want to do the work that goes along with a given role. For example, at the workplace some Gen Xers want the role, but not the responsibility. They expect easy advancement. This certainly became true in Jay King's case—motivated by his family situation, social life, and passion for music, he became less and less responsible at work, missing meetings and dragging his feet on important issues. Boomer dad Paul let this behavior go at first, partly because he himself had given up so much for the businesses he'd launched, but ultimately he called Jay on his lack of commitment and gave him a very real choice to make: the business or everything else.

Now let's consider Comfortable Gen X as a potential symptom in your family business.

Diagnosing Comfortable Gen X

The list below can help you think about whether your family business shows characteristics related to Comfortable Gen X.

IF YOU AGREE MORE THAN DISAGREE WITH THESE STATEMENTS, COMFORTABLE GEN X MAY BE A SYMPTOM WORTH TREATING IN YOUR FAMILY BUSINESS.

- Our business has at least one Gen Xer in a management or other important role.
- There is evidence that Gen X members in important roles aren't always "pulling their weight" with regard to some/all responsibilities.
- The older generations tend to avoid confronting the issue of low commitment in younger generations—or only take action if there's a major problem.
- There is significant conflict or disagreement (especially between generations) over work-life balance—what is worth giving up for work.
- Younger generations in the business tend to be friends with other employees (or have even hired some of them), which leads to management challenges (e.g., unwillingness to confront problem behaviors).
- There are frequent revisions of the "social contract" or expectations of younger-generation members, including as related to responsibilities and work hours.
- Younger-generation members are often out of the office for lunches or other social engagements; sometimes this slows productivity or creates frustration.

Comfortable Gen X: The Treatment

Families must first understand the generation-based patterns they've fallen into and why. Then practical steps are developed to alter these patterns.

Understanding the Stack-Up Patterns

After considering a series of questions about their situation (see Chapter 1), families can begin to understand their specific issues within a context, linking their challenges to underlying sources. For the King family, this meant highlighting the challenges associated with the roles and expectations of family members, especially as related to the typical Gen X issues that Jay was facing: balancing work responsibilities with other very genuine commitments, including family and hobbies. It would be difficult for Jay to turn 180 degrees—from routinely prioritizing some of his other pursuits over work to becoming a "model" manager again—and expecting that to happen wasn't helping anyone. Parents Paul and Roseanne had played a role by accepting Jay's behavior initially—even encouraging it, in Roseanne's case—but then trying to change it wholesale once it had much broader consequences for the business.

The family would also have to acknowledge and confront Carolina's part in the situation. On one hand, it was easy to "blame" her for how Jay had changed: "Jay didn't start acting this way until after he got married," his brother, Will, said. But on the other hand, Jay had to take responsibility for his decisions. Yes, he was stuck between a demanding job and a demanding spouse, but he was an adult and had to learn how to balance these demands; early on, Jay admitted that he felt he had "no choice" in the matter, but that that was an easy excuse. Finally, it's important to recognize the consequences of the situation for Will. Jay's younger brother was struggling to reconcile Jay's low commitment to P.K. with his own responsibilities to the business: if he followed Jay's lead and started slacking off, the business would suffer even more; if he maintained greater responsibility, he would continue to feel that it was unfair for Jay to enjoy such diminished expectations.

Changing the Stack-Up Patterns

Clarify roles and responsibilities. It was clear that Jay had joined the business with little discussion of what his father expected of him. At first this wasn't a problem, as Jay had been motivated to work hard. But subsequently, by having such poorly defined responsibilities, it was easy for Jay to avoid taking much responsibility; in a sense, the family had "colluded" in creating this situation, then had to deal with its negative effects. So now it was critical to define Jay's role and responsibilities much more clearly, and set clear criteria for his success.

Paul and Jay said that they would make this an immediate priority. I encouraged them to use the question "What's best for the business?" in laying everything out. That made it easier to decide new policies. For example, Jay agreed that he'd helped create major issues by hiring friends, taking them away from their responsibilities to help with the music festival, and then dragging his feet when it made sense to lay them off. Father and son agreed to a more mutual hiring process, one that no longer included good friends as candidates. Will's role also needed to become more of a priority. He had less experience and responsibility than Jay, but had already proven his strong commitment to the company, including by voicing his concern about his older brother. Paul and Jay agreed to define Will's role a bit more clearly, and even to have him take on some of the responsibilities that Jay was carrying, to groom him for fast advancement—as long as he earned it.

The idea of clarifying roles and responsibilities pertained not just to the business, but to the family as well. For example, it wouldn't have been prudent to have Jay shift from an excessive focus on the family (and his other pursuits) to over-focusing on his business responsibilities. There were many healthy benefits to Jay's flexibility, including the time he spent with his children and with his wife's extended family. So Jay and Paul also had to take into account the question of "What's best for the family?" Here I suggested that they build greater transparency into Jay's decisions; rather than keeping his plans to himself and disappearing whenever he felt like it—partly to avoid responsibilities at work—he had to let his father and his wife know his schedule. Jay would maintain an electronic calendar that both Paul and Carolina could access. This would diminish greatly the frequency of people having to ask, "Where's Jay?"

Finally we discussed the difficult topic of Carolina's role. By failing to see Jay's work responsibilities as a priority, she had made it a challenge for him to sacrifice family time or his own pursuits for P.K. Construction. She had also cast herself as the "bad guy" for Jay's family, who attributed his behavior almost wholly to her influence. Jay knew that he had to be more upfront with Carolina about what was expected of him at work—as would be defined more clearly going forward—and that he give her a fuller picture of the economic challenges P.K. and the industry more broadly suffered. Carolina admitted that she hadn't realized "how bad" business was, and agreed to try to stop leaving Jay stuck between his obligations to P.K. and to her and the kids.

Create consequences. Part of the reason Jay had been able to slip so much in his responsibilities was that there was little consequence for doing so. The lack of consequences fit with the poorly defined responsibilities—it wasn't clear exactly what Jay was to accomplish, so there couldn't really be rewards or punishments for his performance. Along with laying out clearer responsibilities for Jay and Will, the Kings had to establish clearer compensation systems and career paths for them and others. An example of this need was Jay's resistance to a salary cut at a time when all other managers had accepted one. P.K. couldn't sustain its payroll, given the difficult economic situation, and on top of that it set a bad example to have Jay receive higher compensation than warranted, even if only the family knew about it. After some discussion, Jay agreed that he should have accepted the cut in the first place. Paul said that he would start working on a clearer compensation system with key nonfamily managers and then share this with Jay, Will, and others—and adhere to it.

The idea of establishing consequences also applied to day-to-day and one-off activities. For example, Paul had actually created a consequence for Jay's resistance to laying off his friends: he had brought in another manager to do it, saying, "I can have him take over even more of your work if you'd like." Jay had gotten the message, as the consequence made him look bad in front of his friends and suggested for the first time that he couldn't take his role at P.K. for granted. Paul reported that Jay had become a bit more diligent since that incident, but that there was still plenty of room for improvement.

Because there had been so few consequences in the past, the Kings would be best off using more formal consequences in the short term: all would agree that unless well-defined responsibilities were carried out, the party in question would face specific predetermined outcomes (e.g., loss of pay or responsibility). As time went on and greater trust was built, the family could take a less formal approach. In general, Jay had to learn that there was no "safety net" for his actions—failure to meet obligations would carry penalties, just as in a more typical corporate environment.

Use strengths of differences. Recall that for the Tompkins family of the Generation-Straddling Siblings chapter I suggested leveraging the distinct qualities that each member brought to the situation, whether based on qualifications, interests, or generation. The same advice applies here. Rather than clashing around their points of difference (e.g., Jay's saying, "I'm not going to give up everything for work, like you did" to his father), they had to focus on using the positives associated with each. For example, Boomer Paul brought a work ethic that had helped foster the success of

P.K. Construction, whereas Jay brought a focus on balance that is a hallmark of his Gen X cohort. Neither approach was inherently "bad," but the family's clashes over them had made it difficult to integrate the benefits associated with each. The idea applied to other areas, as well. For example, Jay had always kept his interest in music separate from the workplace, but there were possibilities of merging the two. Rather than putting all of his energy into the music festival, he could have helped bring to life a P.K. Blues Day or similar event, to promote the company to customers and prospects and bring a much-needed morale boost to employees. Paul and Jay liked the idea, and agreed to explore it.

Lastly, brothers Jay and Will had a lot to share with each other, potentially. Unlike Will, Jay had deep experience in financial services, experience that he could have used to excel in his own role. Similarly, Jay could have mentored Will on general management, especially once the older brother renewed his commitment to the business. Will, on the other hand, was a natural hard worker, like his father, and didn't yet have the family responsibilities that Jay did; he and his wife both worked, and their one child, a toddler, was in day care full-time. So Will could have been a good role model for Jay in terms of focusing more strongly on job responsibilities.

Maintaining Changes

Over the next months, Paul and Jay plunged into developing clearer definitions of Jay's responsibilities as general manager in several areas: Profit & Loss, operations, and human resources, for instance. For each area, they made a list of "must-have" activities and "nice-to-have" activities based on market conditions. For the must-have activities, they listed clear, measurable criteria for success. They also linked key criteria to Jay's potential salary increases and bonuses. Given how difficult the construction market was at the time, they agreed that his salary would be frozen for at least the next year—this was a compromise they reached between having Jay accept a pay cut and acting as if it was business as usual (e.g., an expected increase and bonus). In this way they'd driven improvements related to our discussions around clarifying roles and creating consequences—areas that naturally go hand in hand.

They'd also implemented several of the ideas around bringing to the business the best elements of each person's experience. Paul and Jay agreed that they'd stay late together at the office one day a week—something they hadn't done in years—and that Paul would join Jay for a mid-week music event at least once a month. They'd also run with the idea of a P.K. Blues Day, and reported that there was a lot of "excitement" about it among employees—several planned to perform at the event, which featured Jay's band as the headliner.

Despite these improvements, Carolina and Jay still struggled to change her role from pulling Jay from his responsibilities to supporting him in striking a better balance, especially on the occasions when Jay chose business over family obligations. Though Will felt more comfortable with Jay's level of commitment to the business, he and Jay still maintained some distance, largely as a result of the negative feelings that had emerged over recent years. Again my advice was the same: try to empathize and work actively to communicate; failed conversations were better than no conversations at all.

The commitment that the King family showed to making improvements suggested they were well on the way to a more productive business situation and more harmonious family relationships. With time, the question "Where's Jay?" would most likely be replaced with the statement "There's Jay—working hard at P.K., spending time with his family, or strumming his blues guitar."

10

WimpY Gen Y

As parents, it's hard to get it right. Here in the United States, we've gone from communities with no locked doors and children out on the streets at all hours, to a nation with a sharp focus on seat belt laws, cell phones for everyone from an early age, and other safety measures. Of course some of these are necessary and good. But the intensity surrounding the need to protect our children from life's hazards—both physical and emotional—also has significant negative consequences for everyone. Those taking a hard line on the issue have even labeled the country a "Nation of Wimps," based on the youngest generation's inability to do things for themselves—from schoolwork to job responsibilities. It's an especially big challenge for the Gen Y cohort, or Millennials. Naturally these trends represent major challenges for family businesses, where each generation has to be able to step up to lead and take on major responsibilities. Ironically, the very people who depend on later generations to take responsibility are often the ones who've made it hard for them to do that in the first place: the parents, or earlier generation. This chapter helps all generations understand the dynamics and consequences of overprotection on the part of parents, as well as what can be done the reverse its effects.

The Problem with the Prada Princess

From infancy, Sonia Ames needed help. Diagnosed with Type I diabetes, the bright-eyed baby girl required blood tests and insulin daily. Her parents, Martin and Kelly, became experts in the disease and its daily treatment regiment, stocking their southwest Ohio home with books and medical supplies. Largely because of Sonia's diagnosis, Kelly quit her job as an art teacher to stay home with her daughter; of course, dealing with the diabetes didn't take all of her time—Kelly spent a lot of time reading to Sonia, taking her on walks, and going to playgroups. Partly because of the diabetes, Kelly and Martin also decided that they would have no more children.

The parents' attention to Sonia showed in her academic achievement. From the start, she earned high praise from her teachers: "You're doing everything right with her" was a common statement in parent-teacher conferences. Reinforced in this way, Kelly and Martin made sure to check Sonia's homework carefully and enroll her in outside academic programs. As she moved into high school, they advised her on which classes to take to position herself well for college, and spoke frequently to her teachers and guidance counselor. When Sonia received a B in an Honors English class, Martin

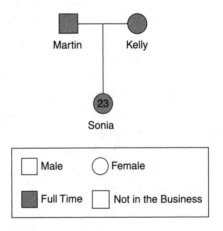

Figure 10.1   WimpY Gen Y: The Ames Family

and Kelly met with the teacher and negotiated for Sonia to redo a key paper, then worked hard with her on it; her grade rose to an A–. Sonia's parents also helped her deal with the ups and downs of nonacademic life. When she suffered a difficult breakup, Kelly took her daughter out for ice cream and told her she was "too good" for her ex-boyfriend. When Sonia got into a car accident while talking on her cell phone, her parents bought her a BMW to replace the totaled car, as a "reward" for her good grades.

Covaledictorian of her class, Sonia was admitted to several colleges both within and outside of Ohio. After the family visited the schools, they decided together that she should attend a private school less than two hours away; it was less prestigious than several she had been accepted to, but gave her the option to come home frequently. It turned out that Sonia didn't return home all that much; instead, her parents came to her. They visited for parents' weekend, of course, but they also came for finals weeks, taking time off from work to help Sonia study and "stay fresh" by doing her laundry and bringing meals to her apartment.

Again the family's hard work paid off: Sonia was recruited by multiple companies, including a major consumer packaged goods corporation in Cincinnati. She took the job. Initially, Sonia thrived in her new job. But soon she was calling her parents to complain about how "stressful" it was, and how some of her managers didn't seem to appreciate her work. Martin offered to talk to her manager for her, but Sonia said that she would "handle" it. A year later, at age 23, she handled it by quitting the job to return home. But not without a new employer in mind: the family business.

The business, Red Aardvark Cards and Design, had started literally at the Ames family's kitchen table. After quitting her art teacher job to stay home with Sonia, Kelly had begun creating greeting cards (some featured a red aardvark cartoon character), decorative photo frames, and other items when Sonia napped or was in school. After several friends expressed interest in buying the products, Kelly convinced several local store-owners to carry them. A buyer for a major discount retailer saw one of the photo frames and approached Kelly about selling them wholesale. Thirteen years later, at the time Sonia wished to join the business, Red Aardvark was a multimillion-dollar company with 50 employees, including CEO Kelly and the head of operations, Martin, who'd quit his job as an engineer to join. Each year, the business donated a portion of revenues to the Juvenile Diabetes Research Fund.

When Sonia suggested she join the family business, her parents were pleased. "We had already worked together in so many ways that it seemed very natural," Kelly said. Given her background and interests, Sonia joined Red Aardvark as a marketing analyst, but was quickly promoted to lead a small team of marketers, all of whom had more experience than she did. Not surprisingly, Sonia's teammates weren't pleased about the new development. But it wasn't just that the boss's daughter had received a premature promotion: Sonia also brought an unwelcome corporate mentality to the relaxed small-company environment, asking her team for frequent updates and calling meetings that many felt were unnecessary. On top of that, she didn't hold herself to the same standard as her teammates, taking frequent time off to shop with friends, go on long-weekend trips, or just to give herself a break. These behaviors—along with driving a BMW to work and wearing designer clothes—earned Sonia the behind-her-back nickname "The Prada Princess."

When one of Sonia's teammates took the risk of hinting about these patterns to Kelly and Martin, it seemed that they either didn't see evidence of a problem or were choosing to ignore it. "She's got a lot on her plate," her father said. "She's got her health to worry about, too," her mother added. End of discussion. But from that point, both parents took pains to be more involved in Sonia's work, often doing it for her—whether sitting in on team meetings or advising her team on new initiatives. Sonia wasn't happy about the new development, and told her parents she could do the work on her own. "It's just until you get settled," Kelly said. Soon, Sonia came to them with a proposal: the business was planning to overhaul their accounting/reporting system, and she wanted to lead the project. When her parents expressed some reluctance, Sonia reminded them that she'd taken several accounting courses in college and been involved in budgeting work for her department at her previous employer.

Kelly and Martin agreed to have Sonia work on the initiative, and asked her to collaborate with the company's head of finance on it. Sonia immediately got to work, contacting several vendors and arranging meetings. She flew to San Francisco to meet with one of the vendors, taking several days off work to fit a vacation in. Sonia returned from California confident that she'd found the best system. When she presented it to her parents and the head of finance, all three raised important issues that Sonia assured them "wouldn't be problems"; after the meeting, the finance head told Martin and Kelly that Sonia hadn't consulted him on the decision. The next day Sonia urged her parents to go ahead with purchasing the system. Though they still had reservations, they signed the contract that Sonia had put together with the vendor.

The new system was a disaster. It was designed to serve much larger companies, and lacked the customization capabilities Red Aardvark needed. When it was clear the system didn't fit their needs, Sonia's parents asked her to look into returning it. She called the company and found out they'd have to pay over $100,000 in penalties, as stipulated in the contract. Rather than taking responsibility for the failure, Sonia blamed her parents, the finance head, and the vendor. "You're not being supportive of my efforts," she told her parents before storming out of the meeting. Kelly and Martin could only look at each other, puzzled and sad that the daughter for whom they'd done so much was acting this way.

WimpY Gen Y: The Symptom

In many ways, parents have never been more supportive of their children than they are now. That's not a bad thing, as the parent-child bond is crucial to the healthy development of each generation. But as the Ames family case shows, too much parental involvement has its downside, and this can become a major problem in a family business situation. I've named this symptom Wimpy Gen Y, but recognize that the name can be misleading. It's important to remember that it's not just about Gen Y's challenges taking on responsibility in multiple domains, but also that earlier generations helped create the problem.

As I'll discuss in a moment, it's a challenge where there's much at stake. Boomers are retiring in unprecedented numbers, and the U.S. needs an "infrastructure" of young managers and employees to fill their shoes effectively. But Boomers and Xers have helped create the problem by overprotecting the next generation. Without measures to mitigate the situation, we'll see far-reaching effects not just for family and nonfamily businesses, but for the U.S. and global economies as well.

Hothouse Parents and the Illusion of Collaboration

In the Comfortable Gen X chapter, we discussed how Gen X can be seen as the "self-esteem" generation because this cohort has been highly focused on finding multiple sources of validation, from family to career to other pursuits. Gen Y (or Millennials), then, may be thought of as the "self-delusional" generation; they are too often given validation without earning it. This is the everyone-gets-a-ribbon generation. Here's a brief example: last month I watched my friend's son compete in a karate tournament for ten-year-olds. On a table were the trophies to be given out: each was exactly the same size, with the place number (from 1st through 10th) inscribed in the tiniest print at the base; there were as many trophies as there were competitors. I asked one of the organizers why the trophies were all the same size and he said, "We wouldn't want anyone to feel bad." That might make sense for toddlers, but these were ten-year-olds expected to "fight" each other!

My point is not that we should make ten-year-olds—or any children—feel bad about themselves. But by taking such pains to protect the youngest generation from difficult emotions, we've prevented them from believing they have to put in any kind of effort to win a reward. They want prizes without even playing, in many cases. When they're older, they want time off without time spent working to earn it. Trends like this have motivated researchers like Hara Marano, editor of *Psychology Today*, to label us a "nation of wimps."[1]

But don't blame the "wimps" themselves. Marano and others are quick to point out who they think is responsible: the parents. In fact, the phenomenon of overprotecting children has yielded terms like "helicopter" and "hothouse" parents. They hover over their kids and build thick barriers between their children and the harsh (and even the just mildly uncomfortable) realities of life, using technology to monitor what the younger generation eats for lunch at school and going with adult children to job interviews, as Marano points out.

In mid-2008, controversy erupted when a *New York Sun* columnist, Lenore Skenazy, allowed her nine-year-old son to ride the New York subway alone from Bloomingdale's in Manhattan to their home. As Skenazy wrote in a column about the incident, "Half the people I've told this episode to now want to turn me in for child abuse. As if keeping kids under lock and key and helmet and cell phone and nanny and surveillance is the right way to rear kids."[2] While Skenazy may be at one extreme among modern parents, too many are at the other, helicoptering and hothousing their children to the point where they grow up lacking life skills and confidence.

It's a trend that starts early and lasts long. Where children used to go outside to find friends—and deal with interpersonal challenges—many of them now stay in and only see peers with whom their parents have arranged "play dates," a term coined only in recent times. Parents today routinely get overinvolved in their children's schoolwork as well, from doing their homework with (or for) them to enrolling them in high-cost tutoring and other education enrichment services (often meeting with the child and the tutor) to ponying up big bucks for SAT classes and college admissions consultants. Part of the problem is that few of us have much confidence in the U.S. public education system; a recent Harris poll showed that fewer than two in ten U.S. adults believe the country provides "excellent" or even "very good" education.[3]

But this trend goes well beyond a lack of faith in educational and other systems. It comes down to a lack of faith in the younger generation to fend for themselves in multiple settings. Ironically, this perception leads to the very problem that older generations fear; having failed to learn from experience, especially that of a negative sort, many Gen Y members are ill-equipped to handle the stresses and strains of school and work. For example, the cycle of oversupport has led to a dramatic spike in students reporting psychiatric problems on college campuses.

Fast Fact

In 2001, 85 percent of North American colleges reported an increase in students with "severe psychological problems" over the past five years.

Source: Hara Marano, "Crisis on the Campus," *Psychology Today,* May 2, 2002 (http://www.psychologytoday.com/articles/200305/crisis-the-campus) (accessed May 25, 2010).

Of course it's a problem at work as well. Too many Millennials are arriving at jobs across sectors without the proper skills—business, technical, and interpersonal—to thrive. It's a combination of an education system that has failed to catch up with the skills needed in today's "Conceptual Age" (e.g., right-brain thinking, empathy, and four other "senses," according to Daniel Pink[4]) and older generations that have done too much of the "work" of life for younger ones. An interesting byproduct of these trends has been an overreliance on collaboration. Yes, collaboration has earned its positive connotations: when done well, it means the whole is much greater than the sum of its parts, as each person contributes something unique from their experience or capabilities. But the downside of working so closely together is that individuals in the collaborative group can hide their areas of deficit and, worse, fail to improve on them when others do the work. A friend of mine is a professor at a premier business school that prides itself on its "collaborative" culture; he told me about a disturbing recent trend. Several employers have complained that the students they hire from the program for full-time work, especially in highly quantitative positions (e.g., finance), seem very qualified on paper and in interviews, but underperform when they actually start the work. My friend blames the trend squarely on the program's emphasis on group work; the more analytically skilled members of the team do the heavy lifting for assignments, but everyone gets the same grade—and the same MBA. So one of the clear trends for Gen Y has been excessive reliance on collaboration to make up for skill and leadership deficits, which only leads to more such deficits.

The stakes associated with Wimpy Gen Y are sky-high, both for the cohort itself and everyone else. Even before the recession that began in 2008, Millennials were amassing debt at an alarming rate, as summed up by a 2010 *USA Today* headline: "Generation Y's Steep Financial Hurdles: Huge Debt, No Savings."[5] The article went on to discuss how nearly 40 percent of Millennials were unemployed or underemployed, with only 58 percent paying monthly bills on time and 60 percent of 20- to 29-year-olds having already cashed out their 401(k)s to cover living expenses. Rising student loan debt and declining employer-covered healthcare and retirement benefits only made the picture bleaker. On top of that, Millennials have inherited a gigantic deficit and a huge Social Security bill, with 10,000 Boomers becoming eligible for the retirement benefit *daily*, as discussed in earlier chapters. Gen Y, children of hothouse parents, are expected to carry the weight of the increasingly older U.S. population without having been given the space to develop the career and life skills they need just to manage their own success.

The Ames family is a textbook example of Wimpy Gen Y. In part because of her early-onset diabetes, daughter Sonia was stifled by her parents' support and protection. Though clearly a bright child, she never had to struggle to gain mastery of key skills. She was helped at every step by Martin and Kelly, whether by being let off the hook for a car accident or having her laundry and meals taken care of during college finals week. So it was no surprise that she failed to meet expectations when she finally faced the challenges of the real world of work. Nor could she or her parents hide her shortcomings when she began to work at Red Aardvark; she took on responsibilities beyond her skills, sidestepped collaboration (in this case, it would have helped), and failed to understand how her actions (e.g., forcing more corporate practices) were affecting her colleagues and their perception of her. When called to task for the first time, she blamed everyone else. In a sense she was right: by spending years protecting Sonia from much of reality, her parents had indeed failed to support her in a more important way—and now they were at a loss for how to do that.

Diagnosing the Symptom of Wimpy Gen Y

The list below can help you think about whether your family business shows characteristics related to Wimpy Gen Y.

IF YOU AGREE MORE THAN DISAGREE WITH THESE STATEMENTS, WIMPY GEN Y MAY BE A SYMPTOM WORTH TREATING IN YOUR FAMILY BUSINESS.

- Our family business has at least one Gen Y member in a management or other important position.
- Parents or other older-generation members tend to be overinvolved in Gen Y members' roles in the business.

- Parents or other older-generation members tend to make excuses for Gen Y members, especially when they are underperforming.
- There is concern that Gen Y members have been given responsibilities that they may not be qualified to handle well and/or that they believe they are entitled to such responsibilities.
- Older and younger generations in the business are surprised when the younger generation fails to step up to major responsibilities.
- Gen Y members have entered (or are likely to enter) the business with little or no outside experience.
- Gen Y members are paid significantly more than their same-level peers, possibly including those with more experience than the Gen Y members have.
- Gen Y members take what some see as excessive time off.
- Gen Y members avoid collaboration or use it to hide skills deficits.

Wimpy Gen Y: The Treatment

Families must first understand the generation-based patterns they've fallen into and why. Then practical steps are developed to alter these patterns.

Understanding the Stack-Up Patterns

After considering a series of questions about their situation (see Chapter 1), families can begin to understand their specific issues within a context, linking their challenges to underlying sources. For the Ames family, this meant highlighting the challenges associated with the roles and expectations of family members, especially as related to the pattern whereby parents Kelly and Martin had done too much for Sonia throughout her life, which became a problem when she took on key responsibilities at the business. Dwelling on history or trying to blame either party for the situation is not helpful; instead, early stages of addressing this symptom should be about understanding why the family is in the predicament they are in and what they can do about it.

Once we developed an initial understanding of the context for their issues, we moved into changing the stack-up patterns to address the symptom of Wimpy Gen Y.

Changing the Stack-Up Patterns

Create a career plan. A big part of the Ames family's problem was that, as thorough as they had been with Sonia at all stages of her life, they had failed to give much thought to one important item: a career plan. This wouldn't have been as much of an issue if Sonia had chosen to have a career outside the family business, but once she joined Red Aardvark, the absence of a career plan became glaring, contributing to numerous challenges. The family needed to come up with a plan for Sonia that involved clear steps and criteria for advancement within the family business.

While the career plan was to include a path to roles involving greater leadership, the family would have to wait until they were absolutely sure that Sonia was ready for more responsibility before placing her in roles that required it. They'd already seen the downside of rushing her into a management role. Taking caution in this area is important for any business, but arguably even more so for family companies, as too-rapid advancement is invariably seen as nepotism, as it was in this case. As such, her advancement plan would be based on merit and credibility, rather than just a set amount of time or small early wins. This would help Sonia and her teams feel much more comfortable about her role.

The career plan could also include something that many family businesses find surprising: outside experience. I can't overstate the value of working somewhere other than the family business before joining it. Many family business leaders report how much family members, especially in later generations, learned through outside experience—whether in regard to functional skills or interpersonal capabilities—which then served them in their family-business roles. Other families express regret about not having made outside experience a requirement for joining the business; they feel that members without external experience too often enter the family business without a frame of reference or a strong enough toolkit. Having Sonia potentially gain more outside experience for a set period of time (e.g., two years) or until she reached a specific milestone (e.g., a promotion to management) represented an opportunity for enrichment, rather than the result of the failure of her initial work with Red Aardvark. Of course, the Ames family had to avoid having the parents involved to any significant extent in any outside job Sonia might take.

Outside experience also helps justify a higher level of compensation for a family member joining the business. Though the family kept it from her co-workers, Sonia had been earning a significantly higher salary than same-level peers, which sends the wrong message whether or not the colleagues are aware of the discrepant compensation. They had to align Sonia's compensation with her title and role, not with her position in the family. They could give Sonia other money as they wished (though it's not advisable in many circumstances), but couldn't consider this part of her Red Aardvark compensation. All of these rules and guidelines had to be discussed explicitly and adhered to carefully by the family as early as possible, ideally before Sonia joined the business.

Look from the outside in. Understandably, Sonia's colleagues were put off by her attitude and even her work attire. They would have felt that way about a nonfamily colleague with the same attributes, but in Sonia's case it was exacerbated by their perception that she was being given preferential treatment. Kelly and Martin's attempts to make excuses just added more fuel to this particular fire.

To approach this issue, the family went through an exercise I call "How Would I See Me?" Each member thinks about their behavior around a certain issue or theme (e.g., team meetings) and then puts themselves in the place of their colleagues, imagining how the behavior would be viewed, especially its negative features. The Ames family went through this exercise both for their behavior as individuals (e.g., Sonia's micromanagement) and as a group (e.g., Martin's making excuses for Sonia's behavior). They struggled with the exercise at first, but slowly began to understand why their colleagues might take issue with some of their behaviors—and even why Prada blouses and other luxury clothing might not have been the best choices for work attire. I urged them to continue thinking about these patterns and eventually to take the next step of soliciting feedback more directly from colleagues.

Collaborate with care. There's a fine line between collaboration and enabling. As discussed earlier, the symptom of Wimpy Gen Y has emerged largely because parents of Millennials have mistaken the latter for the former; they do too many things for their kids, preventing them from becoming independent and confident. Logically, parenting well sometimes means stepping away, even when we know our children are anxious or in emotional pain. At the same time, there are many circumstances where collaboration yields the best outcome. For example, while Martin and Kelly probably shouldn't have been involved in Sonia's college academic experience, it was fine and probably healthy for them to take part in some of her Red Aardvark activities (as long as they weren't taking them over for her) and certainly the right thing for her to collaborate with the finance head on the new reporting system.

So it's about recognizing when collaboration makes sense. I encouraged the family to ask themselves a series of questions when considering a potential collaboration: Is this something Sonia can do by herself? Is there a good learning opportunity in doing this by herself? Why are we *really* getting involved in this—for us or for her? Had Kelly and Martin asked themselves such questions earlier in Sonia's life, they may have been better able to step back and let her learn more lessons on her own. But it wasn't too late to start asking the questions in regard to Sonia's responsibilities at Red Aardvark. Moreover, asking the questions and setting clearer terms for collaboration would help Sonia maintain those boundaries with her parents and other colleagues.

Maintaining the Changes

Over the next several months, the Ames family made good progress; for example, they reported that they'd had several long discussions to lay out a much clearer career plan for Sonia. They said that they'd considered the idea of having her work elsewhere to gain more experience, but decided that her time at the consumer goods company had been sufficient to get a taste of the outside working world. At Red Aardvark, they'd scaled back her management responsibilities, putting her in charge of several special projects in the short term. For each, they'd mapped out who the best collaborators would be, and decided to leave the parents in more of an advisory role, rather than working directly with Sonia on a given initiative. They'd also aligned her compensation more carefully with that of colleagues with the same experience level, and agreed that they could discuss the need for any additional money on a case-by-case basis (e.g., if Sonia moved to a more expensive apartment).

On the dimension of taking a more empathetic perspective toward colleagues, the family reported mixed results. While they understood the need to be more aware of how their behaviors came across, they also felt that it was okay if there was some disparity in how they related to one another versus to coworkers. "We are a family and the owners of the business, after all," Kelly said. But as the owners of the business, they had to do what was best to grow it, which may have meant extra caution about preventing teammates from seeing their actions as motivated by nepotism. They agreed to continue thinking about striking the tricky balance between supporting family members and doing what was best for nonfamily employees.

What impressed me most about the Ames family's attitude was their willingness to reexamine thinking and practices that they'd embraced for so long—literally from Sonia's birth. That openness to new perspectives boded well for their continued progress. And while Sonia was still wearing Prada and other designer clothes to work, I was confident that her colleagues were much less concerned about it, because they were much more comfortable with the family's approach to Sonia's role with Red Aardvark.

11

Surviving Generational Stack-Up Now and Later

We've reached the proverbial end of the road. We've talked about the trends driving generational stack-up in family businesses, the idea that stack-up can be seen as a syndrome, or set of symptoms—each with its own set of associated trends and treatments—and the best approaches to each of the symptoms. And to highlight the symptoms we met ten fictional business families representing amalgamations of the hundreds I've worked with.

So where do we go from here? This last chapter will accomplish two things: (1) help you synthesize what you've learned into elements of a business culture and set of best practices with which to approach symptoms of stack-up *now,* and (2) begin a discussion of the future of generational stack-up, or the family business trends to expect as each existing generation ages and new cohorts enter the picture—and how to handle related conflicts as they arise *later.*

Building Best Practices and a Culture to Handle Stack-Up

We've talked about a lot of different approaches to stack-up symptoms, from clarifying roles and responsibilities to aligning compensation with these; from instituting regular family meetings to spending quality family time together. These are mutually reinforcing practices that apply to multiple symptoms. I encourage you to experiment freely with them, rather than seeing a given treatment as associated only with a given symptom.

In that spirit, I present here a set of core principles and practices to help you approach specific symptoms and the phenomenon of generational stack-up as a whole.

Identify, acknowledge, and clarify roles and responsibilities. Unlike many corporations, family businesses tend to be fast and loose with titles, roles, and responsibilities. After all, it's hard to think of Dad as the COO or Aunt Sally as the president when you've related to them as Dad and Aunt Sally your whole life. On the one hand, that's a good thing for family businesses, as it helps them avoid the rigidness and hierarchy that still characterizes many non-family companies, especially large ones. On the other hand, elasticity with roles and responsibilities can promote sloppy business practices and poor accountability—in both business and family roles. It's easy to pass the buck when it's not clear who was in charge of the buck in the first place. And it might be even easier to fall back into family-based roles and conflicts in a business setting, without even realizing that's what's going on. So a key theme of my work with family business clients is that of understanding and clarifying roles and responsibilities, along with keeping these boundaries clear.

A simple way to think about it is to ask yourself the question, "What is my role here and how should I be playing it to deliver the highest value to the business while not disrupting the roles of others?" It's easy to ask, but a lot harder to answer and even harder to put good answers into practice, especially when members have naturally overlapping and/or broad responsibilities. Sometimes having family businesses fill out role maps that help them place their responsibilities in the context of everyone else's allows everyone to begin to understand points of potential conflict and confusion.

Anticipate points of conflict. Responsibility overlap or confusion is one point of conflict related to generational stack-up in family businesses. But it's not the only one. As the saying goes, forewarned is forearmed. Obviously, this book wouldn't exist if generational boundaries weren't a major source of conflict: intergenerational clashes are major problems for family businesses, as exemplified by the symptoms of Control beyond the Grave, Battle of the Super-Women, Boomer Retirement Mirage, and others discussed earlier.

But just knowing that conflicts happen along generational fault lines isn't enough. The best-prepared families know *how* the conflicts typically play out, and they put thoughtful plans and measures in place to mitigate these or prevent them entirely. For example, older generations tend to push the wisdom of their experience on younger ones—"At your age I was a wife, a mother, and a business owner"—while later generations give earlier ones too little credit for what they've learned and for their skills in certain areas, like technology. More successful family businesses understand that these aren't black or white issues, and that everyone can bring something of value to the business and family. So they tend to have rich, strong relationships within and across generations, bonds that bring out the best in each individual, rather than spur jealousy and other negative feelings. They have family meetings in which individuals can share concerns about the business, their role, and each other, all in the spirit of cooperation and creating the greatest value for the company and the family.

Healthier families also intuitively seem to get the psychological notion of "transference," though they may not even know the term. Transference is the idea that we transfer feelings or ways of relating to close family members to other people in our lives; the classic example might be a man's transferring feelings toward his mother to his girlfriend or wife. In family businesses, we can use a broader definition of the term, as members tend to transfer family relationships (and historical conflicts) to business relationships. When your father is the CEO, you relate to him in a very different way than a nonrelated employee would. And that makes things complicated, especially when tensions arise.

Are you relating to your father as the CEO or as your father or as both? It's not the case that families should avoid transference—and thus the conflicts related to it—altogether. It's more that they understand the complexity of dealing with dual relationships and take steps to address it, whether through open dialogue or working with outside consultants. A good example of this was in the Generation-Straddling Siblings chapter, when Tompkins family members were still relating to one another as they did the last time they all lived together, nearly 30 years earlier. Helping them identify and address that pattern went a long way to improving their issues.

Check in, communicate, and plan. This is another one of those things that sounds like common sense, but is easier said than done. Too many families start with a "foolproof" communication plan, then drop it as soon as conflict arises. The idea isn't that a plan will help avoid conflict altogether, but that a good plan will help a family deal with conflict and learn from it.

Even informal measures can go a long way to maintaining family harmony and business performance. Family business members who are good about checking in with each other, especially during stressful business or family times, tend not to let things get blown out of proportion. A simple "How are you doing with all this?" can be extremely powerful, like presenting a lighted exit sign to someone stuck in a dark room. In this regard, regular family dinners, for both the core and extended families (not always at the same time), can be very valuable. Such dinners can be aimed at discussing business issues, if needed, but mostly at connecting and keeping bonds strong. Another means of bonding is to attend trade shows together, making it a working vacation where the adults can gain valuable business/industry information and contacts and the children can enjoy time together in a new setting.

I generally recommend more formal ways of connecting, in addition to the informal, catch-as-catch-can measures. Here, regular family meetings are a wonderful tool—you can even see them as a powerful weapon for combating family stress and business strain. Again, the core family can meet more frequently, with quarterly or annual meetings for the extended family (in larger business families). Again the theme is both work and fun. Adults set an agenda and talk business, while also setting aside some time for fun activities. The children/cousins focus mostly on enjoyment—of the setting and one another's company—but begin to be more involved in business matters as appropriate, according to age and interest.

There's no magic formula for a family meeting agenda, but there are some principles to keep in mind. For one, it's better to have an agenda than not to, even if it's a simple one. Otherwise, the meeting becomes a potential breeding ground for family and business disputes, or at the very least for the emergence of old and often unhealthy patterns among family members. Another important issue is boundaries—setting them and maintaining them. This may be a boundary regarding when children should and shouldn't be involved in business matters. Or it may have to do with what topics can and can't be discussed at a given meeting. Again, there are no hard rules about specific boundaries, but the idea is to approach meetings strategically and with respect for everyone.

Don't do everything at once. Business families that feel ready to take on issues they're facing often bite off more than they can chew. Don't do that. Though I applaud the ambition of that mentality, it too often leads to more problems than the family started with. One example of this is trying to attack both business problems and family-related problems simultaneously. Yes, they're often related, but trying to focus on both makes it difficult to make progress. Instead, try to circumscribe and define a given problem, then develop a solution to it, one that may have both business- and family-specific elements.

Another situation where simplicity is important is that of a family facing multiple generational stack-up symptoms at the same time. For example, the Brown family of the first chapter was dealing with multiple interrelated symptoms including Who's Your Daddy? and Generation-Straddling Siblings. In general, certain symptoms are much more likely to co-occur, such as Battle of the Super-Women and Meet the MEOWs, or Who's Your Daddy? and Comfortable Gen X. Here, it's tempting to throw as many solutions into the mix as possible; I don't recommend that. Rather, try to look at which symptom or interaction is causing the most stress for the family and/or affecting the business the most, and start with that one. Then, after some progress has been made, reassess the situation and start dealing with remaining symptoms, patterns, or problems.

Again, there's no magic formula or algorithm for deciding what to do. But the more you take a proactive approach to stack-up symptoms and other issues in the family and business, the more sophisticated your solutions will become—and the less problems you'll face in the first place. This is where culture comes in. Many companies—family businesses and others—see culture as some mysterious aura that they either have (often as a result of their founder's approach and/or values) or they don't. They read books and attend seminars and workshops on culture, but still they feel it eludes them. I take a much simpler view: yes, culture is partly about the founder's values and family traditions and the like, but it's mostly about attitude and action—how you think and what you do. Not surprisingly, leaders with more open attitudes toward the family and the business and more proactive approaches to conflicts and other problems tend to have businesses with the healthiest cultures, the least insidious issues, and the best performance. That's all there is to it. So rather than trying to build a specific culture or attending all kinds of workshops on culture, take simple steps and make them standard practice: identify and acknowledge problems; take proactive, strategic approaches to them; acknowledge and learn from mistakes; set rules that make sense for everyone and adhere to them; always be mindful and respectful. If you do all that, I guarantee that you will have a family and business culture that promotes success on every dimension.

Anticipating the Future of Generational Stack-Up

The last section was about how to handle current stack-up symptoms and other issues in your family business. This one is about how to think about future generation-based symptoms and take steps to address them now. No crystal ball is perfect, but there are several safe bets for the future of generational stack-up based on current trends and trajectories. The list of anticipated trends below is by no means exhaustive; it reflects the patterns that I think are most important for family businesses to think about—and begin preparing for.

The wait continues. Stack-up is often about waiting. Because we're all living longer and able to work to a much later age, many businesses are still in the hands of the older generations—the GIs and Silent Generation members—as exemplified by the Control beyond the Grave symptom. Meanwhile, many Boomer, Gen X, and Millennials are waiting to gain responsibility, and the next generation (we don't have a name for it yet) will be joining this long line soon enough. Few of us like to wait, especially when we feel ready for responsibility now. Naturally, that causes stress and conflict within family businesses. So we might think of the Waiting Game as a general symptom of stack-up, and one that will only intensify as more members wait for their time to lead.

As with all the symptoms we've discussed, it's important to understand the dynamics underlying the problem. On the one hand, we know people often strive for leadership positions, and then cling to them once in charge. That means older generations are holding on to power for too long, making younger generations feel crowded. On the other hand, we've observed that Gen X and Y sometimes choose balance over professional advancement, as demonstrated by the Comfortable Gen X symptom. So the question isn't so much about *when* younger generations will get their chance to lead, but about *who* among them is most interested in and capable of leading. It's easy to see how family businesses can fall into the pattern of letting whoever's oldest or most interested take the reins. But that's often a recipe for failure. Instead, families should assess interest and skills early and often, and create clear development plans for those showing the most ambition and promise. These can and should include gaining outside experience before joining the business.

Motivating Gen X and Y. We've already discussed how much of a load Gen X and Y are expected to carry, especially with 10,000 Boomers joining the Social Security rolls daily. I know that I've painted a somewhat bleak picture: the struggle with work-life balance of comfortable Gen X; the mounting debt and unemployment of the Millennials. But there's also a positive side. As Boomers make good on promises to retire or at least share the reins, and typical corporate opportunities continue to diminish, Gen X and especially Gen Y may feel more motivated to step up and take control of their professional destinies—and the family business. Finally moving out of your room in your parents' house, where the rock posters are still on the wall, can be a big incentive. And having fewer choices isn't always a bad thing, as we've seen in the Who's Your Daddy?, Meet the MEOWs, and Comfortable Gen X chapters. Sometimes having fewer paths to choose from helps us pick one and stick with it.

Also, the Millennials are by far the most "wired" generation, even when that means using wireless connections. Social media like Facebook and MySpace have made it easier for Gen Y to maintain many more ties with their peers and others; LinkedIn is leading to knowledge of hundreds of thousands of job opportunities, information that didn't exist for Gen X and older generations. So Gen Y may not have as many professional opportunities as some previous cohorts, but they have access to much more information. That could mean that they'll use it to find opportunities for themselves and for their family businesses—even if that means connecting with outsiders who can help run the business, if they don't want to do it themselves.

Dealing with Gen Next. No one knows exactly what the next generation—the one that's just being born and taking its first steps—will look like. But we do have some clues. More than likely, this will be a smaller generation, coming on the heels of a very large Millennial cohort. It will be a generation with little trust in big business or in big government, given the global recession amidst which it arrived. It will be a cohort that knows not to rely on parents' wealth as a safety net.

On the negative side, this means a more cynical, less trusting Gen Next, one with little faith in economic institutions, including the family. But let's focus on the positives: more than likely, this will be a generation embodying do-it-yourself and entrepreneurship, similar to the business-builders of the 1980s and 1990s (mostly Gen X), but with much greater business and tech savvy. We might also predict a backlash against today's helicopter and hothouse parenting, which means that Gen Next will have the confidence and independence to take real control of their careers and deliver on their ambition.

So what does this mean for family businesses? It could mean taking the time and effort to understand what the next generation is looking for, and creating the space for them to excel in the business (after getting some outside experience). It could also mean preparing for potential conflicts around roles and responsibilities, especially because Gen X and Y, already in "waiting mode," might feel squeezed by Gen Next. Most of all it means following the same MO I've endorsed repeatedly here: assessing existing and potential conflicts, trying to get everyone to understand what drives them— especially generational issues—and working together toward strategic, respectful solutions.

The more things change, the more the solutions remain the same. Things always change. That's part of the joy and frustration of the business world and life in general. If separate generations didn't face economic, social, and cultural changes, they might not have as many clashes, but they also wouldn't have the richness of experience and perspective to draw upon in running their businesses and managing their family lives.

The bigger point isn't to debate the costs and benefits of change but to understand that while you can't anticipate changes on every (or sometimes any) dimension, you can build a mindset and approach to dealing with conflicts that will work in most every situation. Again, there's nothing magical to it; it's about openness to discussion and to taking responsibility, informal and formal communication measures, strategic solutions including some of those in this book, and careful, respectful implementation. Then repeat that when the next issue comes along. The goal, of course, is not becoming a conflict-free family or a complication-free business. The goal is to become a business family that has the confidence, tools, and desire to take on new challenges, generation-based and otherwise, as they arise, always with an eye toward what's best for the business *and* the family.

My hope is that the ideas, perspective, and solutions in this book will help you do that, initially by being willing to believe you can find solutions to stack-up-related problems and subsequently by building a culture and set of practices to best handle them. Good luck as you begin or continue on this journey.

Notes

1 The Syndrome of Generational Stack-Up

1. A longstanding statistic in the field of family business research (see John L. Ward, *Keeping the Family Business Healthy*. Marietta, GA: Business Owner Resources, 1997).
2. U.S. Census data (http://www.census.gov/population/www/ cen2000/briefs/phc-t9/tables/tab07.pdf).
3. CDC data (http://www.cdc.gov/nchs/fastats/lifexpec.htm); WHO data (http://www.who.int/global_health_histories/ seminars/presentation07.pdf).
4. Bureau of the Census. "Older Americans Month: May 2009." (http://www.census.gov/Press-Release/www/releases/archives/ facts_for_features_special_editions/013384.html) (accessed April 15, 2010). B. M. Kestenbaum and B. R. Ferguson, "Number of Centenarians in the United States Jan. 1, 1990, Jan. 1, 2000, and Jan. 1, 2010, Based on Improved Medicare Data." In: "Living to 100 and Beyond," monograph, The Society of Actuaries, 2005.
5. Marc Freedman, *Encore: Finding Work That Matters in the Second Half of Life*. New York, NY: Public Affairs, 2007.
6. Emily Brandon, "How Much Longer Will Aging Boomers Have to Work?" *U.S. News and World Report*, August 11, 2008. (http:// www.usnews.com/money/personal-finance/retirement/ articles/2008/08/11/how-much-longer-will-boomers-need-to-work.html).
7. http://www.ffi.org/user_files/images/rud/2005_fb_us_world. pdf.
8. For example, family business expert John Ward, Director of the Center for Family Enterprise at Northwestern University's Kellogg School of Management, showed that among the largest global businesses, family-controlled firms enjoyed a return on invested capital 30 percent higher than their nonfamily-controlled counterparts (personal communication).

9. Elwood Carlson, "20th Century U.S. Generations," *Population Bulletin*, Volume 64, No. 1, March 2009.
10. Hara Estroff Marano, *A Nation of Wimps*. New York, NY: Broadway Books, 2008.
11. Penelope Trunk, as quoted in "19 Blogs You Should Bookmark Right Now," *Inc.*, November 2009, p. 90.
12. http://www.bls.gov/news.release/youth.nr0.htm (accessed March 19, 2010).
13. "Leviathan Stirs Again," *The Economist*, January 21, 2010 (http://www.economist.com/world/international/display-story.cfm?story_id=15328727) (accessed March 19, 2010).

2 Control beyond the Grave

1. For example, see Stephen Block, *Why Nonprofits Fail: Overcoming Founder's Syndrome, Fundphobia and Other Obstacles to Success*. San Francisco, CA: Jossey-Bass, 2003.
2. CDC Data (http://www.cdc.gov/nchs/fastats/lifexpec.htm); WHO data (http://www.who.int/global_health_histories/seminars/presentation07.pdf).
3. B. M. Kestenbaum and B. R. Ferguson, "Number of Centenarians in the United States Jan. 1, 1990, Jan. 1, 2000, and Jan. 1, 2010, Based on Improved Medicare Data." In: "Living to 100 and Beyond," monograph, The Society of Actuaries, 2005.
4. David Goldman, "Worst Year for Jobs Since '45," CNNMoney.com, January 9, 2009 (http://money.cnn.com/2009/01/09/news/economy/jobs_december/index.htm) (accessed April 4, 2010).

3 Who's (or What's) Your Daddy?

1. See for example Hanna Kokko and Michael D. Jennions, "Parental investment, sexual selection, and sex ratios," *Journal of Evolutionary Biology* 21(4), 2008, pp. 919–48 for a review of biological and evolution-based explanations for divergence in parental roles among males and females.
2. Steven Mintz, "Mothers and Fathers in America." http://www.digitalhistory.uh.edu/historyonline/mothersfathers.cfm (accessed August 18, 2009).

3. Stephan Thernstrom, *A History of the American People*. San Diego: Harcourt Brace Jovanovich, 1984.
4. Barry Schwartz, *The Paradox of Choice*. New York: Ecco, 2003.

4   Battle of the Super-Women

1. Heather Boushey and Ann O'Leary, "A Woman's Nation Changes Everything: Executive Summary," from *The Shriver Report* (http://www.awomansnation.com/execSum.php) (accessed April 11, 2010).
2. The Center for American Progress, "A Woman's Nation Changes Everything," (http://www.awomansnation.com/about.php) (accessed April 11, 2010).
3. Leslie Kwoh, "Female Firms Venture into Male-Dominated Industries and Thrive," *The Star Ledger*, April 11, 2010 (http://www.nj.com/business/index.ssf/2010/04/female_entrepreneurs_venture_i.html) (accessed April 11, 2010).
4. Ibid.
5. Caroline Parry, "Women MBA Applicants on the Rise," *TopMBA*, March 31, 2010 (http://www.topmba.com/articles/women-mba-applicants-rise) (accessed April 11, 2010).
6. The Center for American Progress, "A Woman's Nation Changes Everything," (http://www.awomansnation.com/about.php) (accessed April 11, 2010).

5   Meet the MEOWs—Mommy Executive Officer Women

1. Nicole Santa Cruz, "Women Out-earning, Out-learning Men in More Couples," *Los Angeles Times*, January 20, 2010 (http://articles.latimes.com/2010/jan/20/nation/la-na-marriage20-2010jan20) (accessed April 19, 2010).
2. Heather Boushey and Ann O'Leary, "A Woman's Nation Changes Everything: Executive Summary," from *The Shriver Report* (http://www.awomansnation.com/execSum.php) (accessed April 11, 2010).
3. The Center for American Progress, "A Woman's Nation Changes Everything," (http://www.awomansnation.com/about.php) (accessed April 11, 2010).

4. Nicole Santa Cruz, "Women Out-earning, Out-learning Men in More Couples," *Los Angeles Times*, January 20, 2010 (http://articles.latimes.com/2010/jan/20/nation/la-na-marriage20-2010jan20) (accessed April 19, 2010).
5. Ibid.
6. Ruthie Ackerman, "Women Less Confident When It Comes to Investing," FinancialPlanning.com, February 26, 2010 (http://www.financial-planning.com/news/MassMutual-Sarsynski-Alfred-2665981-1.html) (accessed April 19, 2010); Politics: Jennifer Lawless and Richard Fox, "Why Don't Women Run for Office?" *Brown Policy Report*, January 2004 (http://www.brown.edu/Departments/Taubman_Center/womeninoffice.pdf) (accessed April 19, 2010); Education: "Medical Student Gender and Self-Confidence," *The Medical News*, October 5, 2008 (http://www.news-medical.net/news/2008/10/05/41802.aspx) (accessed April 19, 2010).
7. http://www.womensheart.org/content/HeartDisease/heart_disease_facts.asp (accessed April 19, 2010).
8. Candice Watters, "The Cost of Postponing Childbirth," TroubledWith (http://www.troubledwith.com/Transitions/A000000611.cfm?topic=transitions%3A%20having%20a%20baby) (accessed April 19, 2010).
9. David Brown, "Life Expectancy Drops for Some U.S. Women," *Washington Post*, April 22, 2008 (http://www.washingtonpost.com/wp-dyn/content/article/2008/04/21/AR2008042102406.html?sid=ST2008042102630) (accessed April 19, 2010).
10. "Women's Life Spans Drop in Poor Corners of U.S.," MSNBC.com, April 22, 2008 (http://www.msnbc.msn.com/id/24255060/ns/health-aging/) (accessed January 2, 2010).
11. Lynne Lancaster and David Stillman, When Generations Collide. New York: Harper, 2002.

6 Boomer Retirement Mirage

1. Chavon Sutton, "The 60-plus Set Can't Afford to Retire," CNNMoney.com, March 3, 2010 (http://money.cnn.com/2010/03/03/pf/retirement_delay/index.htm) (accessed April 25, 2010).

2. Emily Brandon, "Retirement Savers Lost $2 Trillion in the Stock Market," *U.S. News & World Report*, October 8, 2008 (http://www.usnews.com/money/blogs/planning-to-retire/2008/10/08/retirement-savers-lost-2-trillion-in-the-stock-market.html) (accessed April 25, 2010).

3. Chavon Sutton, "The 60-plus Set Can't Afford to Retire," CNNMoney.com, March 3, 2010 (http://money.cnn.com/2010/03/03/pf/retirement_delay/index.htm) (accessed April 25, 2010).

4. See, for example, Phyllis Moen, Donna Dempster-McClain, and Robin Williams, "Successful Aging: A Life-Course Perspective on Multiple Roles and Women's Health, *American Journal of Sociology*, 97(6), May 1992, pp. 1612–38.

5. Hillary Waldron, "Links between Early Retirement and Mortality," Working Paper, Social Security Administration Office of Policy, August 2001 (http://www.ssa.gov/policy/docs/workingpapers/wp93.pdf) (accessed April 25, 2010).

6. Anna Rappaport and Terry Kozlowski, "Future Patterns of Work and Retirement," World Future Society Presentation, July 2009 (http://www.wfs.org/wfs2009RetirementPDF.pdf) (accessed April 25, 2010).

7. Walter Updegrave, "What You Really Need in Retirement: Friends," CNNMoney.com, February 17, 2010 (accessed April 25, 2010).

8. "Leviathan Stirs Again," *The Economist*, January 21, 2010 (http://www.economist.com/world/international/display-story.cfm?story_id=15328727) (accessed March 19, 2010).

7   My Child, My Boss

1. Moya Mason, "Worldwide Business Startups" (http://www.moyak.com/papers/business-startups-entrepreneurs.html) (accessed April 30, 2010).

2. "Kaufman Study: Number of New Businesses Rises," September 22, 2005 (http://www.bizjournals.com/kansascity/stories/2005/09/19/daily31.html) (accessed April 30, 2010).

3. The Kaufman Foundation, "Number of New Companies Created Annually Remains Remarkably Consistent Across Time," January 12, 2010 (http://www.kauffman.org/newsroom/

number-of-new-companies-created-annually-remains-remarkably-constant-across-time-according-to-new-kauffman-foundation-study.aspx) (accessed April 30, 2010).

4. Sharon Jayson, "Gen Y Makes a Mark, and Their Imprint is Entrepreneurship," *USA Today*, December 8, 2006 (http://www.usatoday.com/news/nation/2006-12-06-gen-next-entrepreneurs_x.htm) (accessed April 30, 2010).

5. Alana Klen, "Dorm-room Business Can Launch Career," Bankrate.com (http://www.bankrate.com/finance/money-guides/dorm-room-business-can-launch-career-1.aspx) (accessed May 1, 2010).

8 Generation-Straddling Siblings

1. Stepfamily.org, quoting 1990 U.S. Census (http://www.stepfamily.org/statistics.html) (accessed May 6, 2010).

2. Glen Olsen and Mary Lou Fuller, "Facts and Myths about Blended Families," education.com (http://www.education.com/reference/article/facts-myths-about-blended-families/) (accessed May 6, 2010).

3. Frank Sulloway, "Birth Order, Sibling Competition, and Human Behavior." In Paul S. Davies and Harmon R. Holcomb, eds., *Conceptual Challenges in Evolutionary Psychology: Innovative Research Strategies*. Dordrecht and Boston: Kluwer Academic Publishers, 2001, 39–83.

9 Comfortable Gen X

1. Lynne Lancaster and David Stillman, *When Generations Collide*. New York: HarperCollins, 2002.

2. Economic Mobility Project, "Economic Mobility in America: Is the American Dream Alive and Well?" July 2008 (http://www.economicmobility.org/reports_and_research/other?id=0003) (accessed May 18, 2010).

3. Alison Damast, "MBA Job Outlook Improving," Bloomberg Businessweek, February 3, 2010 (http://www.businessweek.com/bschools/content/feb2010/bs2010021_018515.htm) (accessed May 17, 2010).

4. Bureau of Labor Statistics, "Economic News Release: Employee Tenure Summary," September 26, 2008 (http://www.bls.gov/news.release/tenure.nr0.htm) (accessed May 17, 2010).

5. Shirleen Holt, "Workaholics Glad to Labor While Others Play," *Seattle Times*, September 4, 2004 (http://seattletimes.nwsource.com/html/businesstechnology/2002027666_doers06.html) (accessed May 17, 2010).

6. Lynne Lancaster and David Stillman, *When Generations Collide*. New York: Harper, 2002.

10   WimpY Gen Y

1. Hara Marano, *A Nation of Wimps*. New York: Broadway Books, 2008.

2. Mike Celizic, "Mom Lets 9-year-old Take Subway Home Alone," MSNBC.com, April 3, 2008 (http://today.msnbc.msn.com/id/23935873/) (accessed May 25, 2010).

3. "Harris Poll No. 45: Few Adults Give High Marks to the Nation's Public Schools for Quality of Education," Harris Interactive, June 2, 2006 (as cited in Harris Interactive, *Trends and Tudes*, Volume 7, Issue 2, March 2008) (http://www.harrisinteractive.com/vault/HI_TrendsTudes_2008_v07_i02.pdf) (accessed May 25, 2010).

4. Daniel Pink, *A Whole New Mind*. New York: Riverhead, 2005.

5. Christine Dugas, "Generation Y's Steep Financial Hurdles: Huge Debt, No Savings," *USA Today*, April 23, 2010 (http://www.usatoday.com/money/economy/2010-04-23-1Ageny23_CV_N.htm) (accessed May 25, 2010).

Index

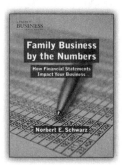
th Family Business Leadership publication is packed cover-to-cover
 expert guidance, solid information and ideas that work."

—Alan Campbell, CFO, Campbell Motel Properties, Inc., Brea, CA

ile each volume contains helpful 'solutions' to the issues it
rs, it is the guidance on how to tackle the process of addressing
different issues, and the emphasis on the benefits which
stem from the process itself, which make the Family Business
ications of unique value to everyone involved in a family
ness—not just the owners."

—David Grant, Director (retired), William Grant & Sons Ltd.
(distillers of Glenfiddich and other fine Scotch whiskeys)